EUGENIO BACCHION

D0534679

The Basilica of
ST. MARK

Translated by Gianni Zanmarchi

⬣ ARDO/EDIZIONI D'ARTE/VENEZIA

SUMMARY

PROPRIETA' LETTERARIA E ARTISTICA RISERVATA
COPYRIGHT © 1972 BY ARDO/EDIZIONI D'ARTE/VENEZIA

THE BASILICA OF ST. MARK

MITH · LEGEND · HISTORY

The Basilica of St. Mark is a miracle brought about by the joint action of heaven and earth, the East and the West.

That is the impression we have when we enter the Basilica after crossing the portico which is an initiation into the mystery. Our eyes still dazzled by the outside brightness, we suddenly find ourselves wrapped in a mystical pathos arising from the lights and shadows that play between the spaces and solids and change continually according to the time of day, and from the iridescent colours that ascend from every side and converge into the often glittering and at times subdued gold of the vaults and cupolas. The interior is dominated by the Cross and the Apostles of the iconostasis, aligned as if in a holy conversation-piece whose centre is the sign of the Redemption; and if the death of the Lord is the subject of the catechesis, the triumphant Christ (Pantocrator), king of the visible and invisible universe, enthroned in the vault of the apse, is the *alfa* and *omega* of human and divine history; he is supported from beneath by the figures of the four protectors of Venice, Nicholas, Peter, Mark and Ermagora.

Here the Divine Spirit hovers everywhere like a cloud over the Holy Ark, symbolized by the hundred little flames burning in the large cross that does not hang from the cupola of the Pentecost by chance. In St. Mark's there palpitates a vibrating soul which fills us with quickening pulsations, for it is a source of life.

The sacred poem begins in the portico, whose mosaics sing the hymn of the creation and celebrate the deeds of the chosen people from which the scion of the root of Jesse (Jesus) was born; it then unfolds itself inside the Basilica with the figures of the Virgin, the Patriarchs, the Prophets, the Saints, and the Martyrs and concludes its mystery in the new heavens and new earths announced by the iconography of the vault of the Apocalypse.

We can immediately grasp here the very essence of the Christian message and of the liturgy which celebrates the perennial jubilation of the Church.

In the Basilica of St. Mark, like in early Cristian churches or in churches of the Ravenna and Romanesque types, the soul feels deeply touched: even the unbeliever finds himself enveloped in an atmosphere which is not of this world, like the wind that stirs Dante's divine forest. And the earth has responded to this heavenly intimation, for the human genius has crystallized its inspiration and its feelings which give life to Faith for eternity.

The East and the West, I wrote. It is true that St. Mark's was built with whatever material could be supplied by the dead cities of the nearby mainland as a memorial of their glorious past, but it is no less true that two civilizations are here interwoven into a creative originality that knows no equal.

Byzantium seems to dominate with its cupolas surmonted by decorative and pictorial Greek crosses, its typical mosaic decoration, and its architectural structure which finds so many peerless models in Constantinople. But the spirit of the West, then in the process of being crystallized had been offering its contribution from the very beginning, enriching the Basilica with stylistic, decorative and figurative elements that bear the hallmark of its genius. The great central doorway with the storied arches in the style of Antelami is one very powerful western note among the many others.

It is commonplace to say that Venice, born of the sea like Venus, is a city of dream and a city of love. Only a poet, then, can understand her, and the myths and legends which accompany her genesis are pure poetry.

Cold intellectualism mortifies, and, also in these hard times, leave us alone in our boat, gently adrift on the tides of the lagoon and immersed in the vision of a boundless sky reflecting itself in the waters and the contemplation of a landscape which, with its islands and distant shores, conjures up to us images of a bygone past, in a silence which is like the siren's song. Ammiana and Costanziaca, where do you sleep?

I can understand the demands of science; but if it has the power to destroy visions, images and feelings and reject the voices that come from afar, then science frightens me, for only the imagination can give Venice and her lagoon the charm which continues to be the essence of her mirage. Myths and legends are not history but the choral expression of the innermost nature of the people, who believe in them because they satisfy the demands of their prophetic and religious spirit.

One day God set his eyes on the place where Venice was to rise and on that day there was light. Then he uttered these sacramental words: « *Marcus habet terras, Marcus habet mare, sidera Marcus* ». Mark, this is the name; and in the century when the Church was born the nations saw Mark and Ermagora on the road to Aquileia where they had been sent by Peter to preach the Gospel. Ermagora was made bishop of Aquileia and Mark left him behind and set sail towards new lands for his apostolic pilgrimage. Tempest-tossed, Mark repaired to the Rialto islands and there fell asleep; in his sleep he had a vision: an angel appeared to him and hailed him: « *Pax Tibi Marce Evangelista Meus* », and then announced to him that in those islands he would sleep the sleep of the just till Judgment Day. This dream is probably represented in the marble group in vigorous Romanic style situated in the lunette of the doorway to the narthex.

The angel's salutation to Mark was the flag the Serenissima was to unfurl through all the vicissitudes of her history. « Long live St. Mark! » was the cry of humiliated Venice in 1797. « Long live St. Mark! » was the cry of Venice breaking the chains of foreign domination in 1848. Daniele Manin, the Tyrtaeus of the insurrection, stands under an arch by the Flower Doorway.

The islands of the lagoon form a constellation at a short distance from the mainland. Were they inhabited at that time? There is no doubt that an indigenous population had been living here since the days of the late Roman Empire, gradually increasing in number on account of the immigrations caused by the storms of the barbaric invasions. Once the hurricane was over the greater part of the refugees returned to where they had come from, but many remained and settled here definitively, thus contributing to the increment of the civil and economic life of the community.

Cassiodorus gives us an idyllic and picturesque view of the customs of these pioneers. Speaking in King Vitiges' name, he asked the people of the Venetian lagoon to take wine and oil safely from Istria to Ravenna, since they possessed « a large number of vessels »: « Your ships do not fear the rough winds and reach land with the greatest ease... their hulls being sometimes invisible, they seem to drift through the meadows. Over there are your houses, now on the mainland now on the islands, like those of waterfowl... dwellings that were not supplied by nature but built by the care of men who, binding the earth with pliant osiers, set this frail bulwark against the billows of the main. You have abundance only of fish, and, rich and poor, you live in equality; only in the salt-works is there competition among you; instead of ploughs, instead of scythes, you turn cylinders; you art rules over every wave, for salt is like edible money; men can dispense with gold, but there is no one who can do without salt ».

These Venetians, then, were frugal, skiful seafaring men: « when you traverse these infinite spaces you are sailing across your real home ».

They braved the open sea in order to trade, to transport goods and hire out their ships. The gulf which stretches from Grado to the mouths of the Brenta, the Adige and the Po is full of hidden dangers owing to its shoals, its uncertainly laid-out and ever-changing routes, and its insidious winds, but it forms a safe dwelling-place, and one can sail over « the seven seas » as if one were at home; here, Cassiodorus wrote, is the home of a people entering history with distinctive features of their own.

Out of this *humus*, which reminds us of the island of Phaeacia, a flower was destined to grow.

Venice has fixed March 25th, 421, Lady Day, as her *dies natalis*. A church is supposed to have been the first sign of the settlement of a community on the Rialto islands; only a legend, to be sure, but there is no evidence to disprove the assumption that the refugees, by then converted to Christianity, may have built churches on the islands of the lagoon, one of them where today the Rialto stands, and that the date of its foundation may have been fixed much later. Once she became great, Venice accepted this tradition; the day was solemnized, and Our Lady of the Annunciation was honoured with particular devotion. It would be difficult to mention the countless figurative representations of this mystery, but the Basilica itself is enriched by it: in the two small kiosks at the farthest ends of the façade there is the Angel of the Annunciation (the Northern one) and in the one to the South is the Virgin absorbed in prayer, receiving the message. On top of the spire of the Campanile there towers the Archangel Gabriel, one hand holding the lily and the other lifted and stretched out towards the angelic words: *Ave Maria*.

Today Venice celebrates her *dies natalis* because of its nostalgic charm. On Lady Day the statue of the Virgin in

Page 5 - A comprehensive view of the Venetian lagoon as it probably looked in the first centuries of our story.

the square in front of the station is decked with flowers as an omen of abounding life: that is the significance of the ceremony according to the late Pope John.

The Basilica of St. Mark was the flower which grew out of the interrelated political, social and religious events that characterized, often with fierce and bloody struggles, the gestation of the Serenissima. I ought perhaps to dwell briefly on the subject.

The phantom of Attila, « *flagellum Dei* », is still alive in the minds of simple people, who are ready to believe that a rustic marble seat at Torcello is the old throne of the King of the Huns. But rather than the invasion of Attila, which populated Grado and Torcello by destroying Aquileia and Altino, the immigration from the mainland to the lagoon islands was really caused by the Longobard invasion, especially after Rothari had extended his conquests to the municipal cities of the Veneto area, which had still enjoyed some show of freedom. The people, whose influx had never ceased, now settled definitely in the islands of the lagoon; 638 is a milestone in the history of the lagoon, for the foundation of Civitas Nova Eracliana (Eraclea) was destined to inspire D'Annunzio's *The Ship*, which the poet symbolically set afloat on the sea as an omen of the Empire of the Venetians. The Venetian lagoon, together with a small strip of the coastal area, formed part of the Ravenna Exarchate, and the latter was certainly Byzantine territory, like Istria and Dalmatia. But the immigrants formed well-knit communities, with a civil and religious life of their own, and they possessed independent customs and traditions and a fully developed civilization, whose roots lay in juridical and social institutions and in moral and religious factors that were Veneto-Roman. Fleeing from the foreign invaders, they wanted to shape their destiny with their own hands.

In the sixth and seventh centuries the communities were governed by Tribunes elected by the *civitas* and chosen among the chief citizens; this took place with the formal approval of Byzantium. But the regime of the tribunes accentuated the growing civil and political indepedence of the Venetians, before a sovereign authority that was getting weaker and weaker, while its decisions were more and more disregarded, even if not yet openly rejected.

It was not a golden age. The high-handedness of those wielding power, the rivalries of interests and the pride and ambition of individuals and classes brought about a series of violent struggles. An even if they were not strong enough to exert absolute authority, the Byzantines could easily exploit the situation by underhand plots and intrigues in order to reinforce their regime, control the seething situation and keep hold on those who threatened to break loose from their nets.

Religion was part of this incandescent situation; the bishop, *defensor civitatis*, played an important role in public life. Acting as the people's protector from the abuses of power and the severity of the local magistrates, he enjoyed great prestige because of his moral authority as well as his ministry. In the sixth century Christianity was rent by the so-called schism of the Three Chapters. Justinian's condemnation of certain writings by Theodore of Mopsuestia, by Teodoreto, and Iba, bishop of Edessa, loosely inspired by Nestorius' doctrine, was accepted by the Council of Constantinople in 553 but rejected by many bishops, especially those of the North Adriatic, who believed that it questioned the doctrine officially sanctioned at Chalcedon. In short, this intricate question ended with the creation of two metropolitan sees, one at Aquileia, with the episcopal churches of the Longobard Venetia suffragant to it, and the other at Grado, which was called Nuova Aquileia because it had given shelter to Patriarch Paolino, controlling the bishops of Istria and the islands subjects to the Byzantine Empire. These events led to the separation of the maritime Venetia from the western territories, and in one way religious autonomy favoured the political independence of the lagoon, which was scattered with episcopal sees: Caorle, Eraclea, Jesolo, Torcello, Malamocco, and the see of Olivolo (San Pietro in Castello). Obelerio, son of Emogino, Tribune of Malamocco was, according to tradition, the first bishop of the Rialto islands; a residential bishop, unlike his predecessors, who had taken shelter in the islands only temporarily and afterwards had all returned to their sees. Padova, Altino, Oderzo, Concordia Sagittaria had left their mark.

The itinerant apostles are now crowned with the halo of glory: Eliodoro, Liberale, Magno, Tiziano, Ermagora, Fortunato, Teonisto, Tabra, and Tabrata, the last five from Aquileia, form a constellation in the firmament of the lagoon.

It must not be forgotten that Venice was born Benedictine.

The monks played a very important role in the complex life of the *civitas*. There were many Benedictine *insulae*, and the one which acquired the greatest renown was the Abbey of Sant'Ilario, founded at the time of the Partecipazi as a daughter church of San Servilio. It stood on the mainland behind Fusina, but no trace of it is left.

In the ninth and tenth centuries state decisions were taken here, and men of high repute and with heavy responsibilities found peace, serenity and light. Five doges chose the Abbey as their burial-place and it was here that Vidale Candiano, brother of the unfortunate Pietro Candiano IV, took the Benedictine vows and died after abdicating from the supreme office of the Republic.

The ecclesiastical and religious framework acted no doubt as a restraining influence in the dispersion of the political energies that were trying to achieve a precarious balance. It was as a consequence of these exigencies that the office of doge was apparently born. Tradition has it that the first doge was Paoluccio Anafesto, elected at Eraclea by a free popular assembly, but his is an unsubstantial figure, blurred by the thick mists of time. The territory ruled by the doge rose to the status of a definitively established national entity at the time of the iconoclastic movement, when the Italian territories subject to Byzantium refused to accept the Emperor's decree prohibiting the cult of sacred images. In 726 Orso was elected doge, and it is his election that marks the certain beginning of the high office, which still recognized the authority of Byzantium. After about two deades doge Deodato transferred the seat of government from Eraclea to Malamocco, which was considered a safer place; further from the savage struggles that were then raging in the lands of the lagoon.

The collapse of the Longobard and Byzantine rule in Italy as a result of the Frank conquest and the struggles between Franks and Greeks for supremacy on the Adriatic helped to bring about the political independence of the Venetians, who could not, however, avoid the dilemma of whether they had to look towards the East or the West. Hence the uncertainties, hesitations and contradictions which encouraged Pépin to invade the lagoon area in order to bring the Adriatic under Frank control. But the Venetian nation reacted with firmness and decision

Aerial view of St. Mark's Square.

and defended the freedom of the lagoon both from the Frank invasion and the aims of the Byzantines, who could have exploited the situation.

Owing to the confused and bloody feuds mentioned above, Malamocco, the new political centre, did not have an easy life. After Pépin's unsuccessful attempt, and apart from the fact that the two Empires had agreed upon a compromise, the territory of the lagoon represented a barrier precluding any further Frank progress towards the sea and keeping alive the last Byzantine phantom in the North Adriatic.

In 811 the seat of the government was transferred from Malamocco to the Rialto by Agnello Partecipazio. It was a wise decision, suggested by a series of internal and external events, and it marked a step forward in the social and political evolution of the lagoon. At that time the Eastern Empire was violently shaken by dark court intrigues, as a result of which the throne fell into the hands of the Empress Irene, who had her young son Constantine IV blinded out of sheer thirst for power. These events facilitated the birth of the Western Empire by the banks of the Tiber. In 800, on Christmas night, Charlemagne was acclaimed Emperor by the people and crowned by Pope Leo III in St. Peter's.

The family of the Partecipazi (Agnello, Giustiniano and Giovanni) held the dogal office for about three decades, and it is written that they « governed Rivalta as Tribunes for hundreds of years, and the court where they administered justice was at Santi Apostoli »; some buildings in the Campiello della Cason, in which traces of those distant times are still visible, are commonly believed to have been the seat of the Tribunes' government.

In 828, during Giustiniano Partecipazio's office, the venerable relics of St. Mark were taken from Alexandria to the Rialto by the merchants Buono da Malamocco and Rustico da Torcello. It this legend or history? It is difficult to answer with certainty. In my opinion the fact is unquestionably true, for it touched the innermost Christian soul of an entire people, and the emotions can never be stirred thus by a phantom or a fable. And even if St. Mark was the right man who came at the right time I refuse to believe that it may have been all a trick contrived for cunningly calculated political reasons.

St. Mark's body was the symbol of Venice. At first it was kept in a chapel of the Palace, and then it was removed to a church which had soon been built next to it; this church went down in history with the name of Basilica of the Partecipazi.

Aquileia and Grado, the New Aquileia, could no longer continue with their reciprocal excommunications on the grounds that each was the sole heir to the Evangelist's authority. Now St. Mark spoke only in Venice, which possessed his body and found strength in his spirit.

The importance of this event is obvious. For his associations with the old « Pax Tibi Marce » legend, St. Mark was, in the sensitive soul of the Venetians, the expression of a robust even if ingenuous religious feeling, while the motto « Fortissimus Leo » was a reminder of their dignity and national conscience. This brought about a sort of symbiosis of political and religious values between St. Mark and the Serenissima, so that on certain occasions the Venetian church acquired a truly national character. The alliance between St. Mark and Venice was concluded: « Ti con nu, nu con ti ». (You with us and we with you). The inscription in the great vault above the sepulchre reads as a law: « Italiam Libiam Venetos sicut Leo Marce doctrina tumulo requie fremituque tueris ».

Page 9 - A harmonious and solemn view of the present Basilica. ▶

THE BASILICA OF THE PARTECIPAZI AND THE ORSEOLI

According to the old chronicles, in the VI century Narses had a church built in the Rialto area in honour of St. Theodore, who had been a soldier and a martyr in the Black Sea region under the reign of Diocletian, and whom afterwards popular imagination promoted to be an officer and made die at Eraclea. St. Theodore, a Greek, became the protector of the Venetians, and he remained so even after the arrival of the Latin St. Mark, but the outline of his figure grew gradually more and more indistinct, though the Serenissima had his statue placed on one of the columns in the Piazzetta.

When the Basilica of St. Mark was begun, the church of St. Theodore disappeared to make room for « Missier San Marco ».

What exactly do we know about the basilica of the Partecipazi? What were its structure and ornaments like? Some would have it built in wood, which would explain the fires that practically destroyed it. According to others it had a simple basilica plan, in the manner of the churches built at Ravenna during the exarchate. And there are others still who maintain that it was built on a cruciform plan, and that it was solemnly decorated according to the pattern of the oriental churches in Constantinople. The dispute will probably never come to an end; I take no side, because I am no authority on the subject. Since in those days life was a rather miserable and sad affair I imagined something simple and unpretentious; but then I no longer felt sure after looking at the superb cathedral at Torcello, which was built in the VII century, and at the solemn, severe cathedral at Caorle — this,

An ancient mosaic in the cove of St. Alipio. The relics of St. Mark are carried into the Basilica, whose XIV century façade is here reproduced.

A detail of the façade of the Basilica with the triumphal arch and the loggia called « of the horses ».

▶

however, is rather late — with its cylindrical campanile in the Ravenna style, with its smaller edition at Tessera. The church of the Partecipazi, consecrated in 832, was almost completely destroyed by a fire which, starting from the Ducal Palace, spread over a large adjacent area. The people had risen against Pietro Candiano IV's tyranny. His successor, Pietro Orseolo the Saint, repaired the heavy damage to the building, preserving, however, its original shape and embellishing it with marble and stone facings taken from Altino, Oderzo and Concordia. The new church was consecrated in 978. It was called St. Mark of the Orseoli after the rulers who had promoted its restoration and decoration.

The Orseoli were at the height of their power at the end of the X century and the beginning of the XI. Pietro Orseolo II, the doge whose name is linked with a successful far-seeing policy, is celebrated for his repeated victories over the pirates infesting the Adriatic and for his conquest of Dalmatia. Out of these events rose the tradition of the splendid ceremony of the marriage of Venice with the sea: « *Desponsamus te, mare, in signum veri perpetique dominii* ».

The Saint whose name is linked whit St. Mark's church had a difficult life as a doge, and this, together with his piety and other Christian virtues, induced him to renounce the high office and end his days in the Benedictine abbey of Cuxa, in the Pyrenees. Cardinal Patriarch Angelo Giuseppe Roncalli (later Pope John) who was always deeply attracted by Venetian history, made it the object of a pilgrimage.

Tentative reconstruction of the plan of the Basilica of the Partecipazi.

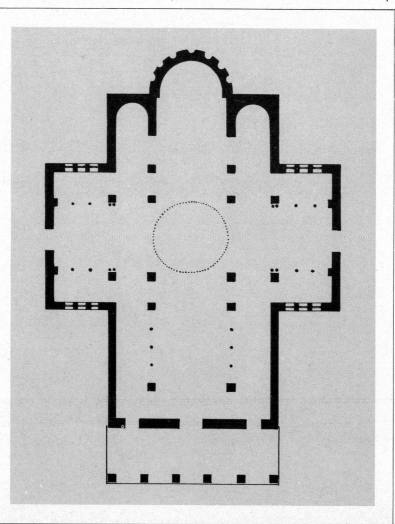

Is there any evidence or document in the present-day Basilica which somehow connect it with the church of the Partecipazi and the Orseoli?

I have no doubt that the decorative elements in the lunette above the door of Saint Alipio enclosed by an Arab-Moorish arch belonged to the church of the Partecipazi-Orseoli; the five small pierced windows in Byzantine style are of exquisite workmanship. The same ornamental motive can be found also above the window giving light to the Zen Chapel; this very charming composition was obtained by piecing together old and precious materials salvaged from the demolished building.

The columns, capitals and paterae we admire today could also be admired then. The interior and the exterior of the Basilica are decorated with many panels — one is reminded here of Ruskin's *Stones of Venice* — that were cut in different ages and taken from different buildings; some of them have been squared and carved before the year one thousand, or may even go back to a period previous to the erection of the first church. Giustiniano Partecipazio's will contained an injunction to his wife to supervise the construction of the Basilica and to use « *de lapidibus* » which could be taken from the Casa Teofilato at Torcello. We feel justified in assuming that materials from the old Roman municipia were employed as well — especially in the foundations. The sacred relics of the dead cities must have filled some Caius Marius wandering among them with a feeling of wonder and regret, but also of pride, such as is today called up by the sight of the *exuviae* in Roman forums.

The gonfalon of St. Mark with the cupolas in the background.

An important archaeological discovery — parts of a monument of a soldier with shield, spear and greaves — was recently made in the crypt of the Basilica, in the foundations of the north wall. It dates back to the Augustan age and came originally from Altino; it is now stored in the cloister of Sant'Apollonia.

Of particular interest are the early medieval marbles decorating the present Basilica and mostly along the galleries and the steps leading to the left ambo. On one of them is carved a so-called star of David: was it a whim of the stone-mason or is it evidence of its place of origin?

Critics divide these panels into three groups: the first includes those presenting an identical iconographic motive, expressed in the Chrismon with ribbons and crosses; the second is characterized by osier mouldings; the third by the prevalence of the motive of the ribbon in the composition. We can safely assume that many of these panels, plutei and screens once decorated the churches of the Partecipazi and the Orseoli. I want to describe one among them which seems to me strikingly expressive: it is a Greek marble pluteus of remarkable size, situated in the gallery to the left of the nave. In the centre there is Christ's monogram, surrounded by a laurel crown from which start two streamers terminating in a heart and reaching the bases of two deeply engraved lateral crosses; the pattern is completed by two burning candelabra at each end. It dates back to the first half of the sixth century and it shows the influence of the Ravenna style.

What can we read in these rugged signs? It is a cryptic catechesis. Christ, God's *uiòs*, is one with the glory of the Father; the true God, He was born of the true God, and the crosses connected with the laurel crown symbolize the redemption of Man through His sacrifice; the two candelabra represent the Faith of the believers; Man is saved through his Faith in God. But the candelabra are also prophetic symbols; Christ is the light that will burn through eternity, as was foretold by the prophets, and as is celebrated in the Easter liturgy when the deacon announces the mystery of the Resurrection in the dark night by repeating the words « *Lumen Christi* » and then lighting the Paschal candle while he sings the victory hymn « *Exultet* ».

The basilica of the Partecipazi and the Orseoli was an object of loving care for three centuries, during which time many decorative and chromatic elements — sometimes in the shape of long terracotta or stone friezes — were added to embellish and enrich the building. Many fragments dating from those times are to be found in the lapidary museum of Sant'Apollonia. Several of them are still black with the smoke of fires that broke out in that dark age, maybe of the very fire which, after destroying the Palace and the temple, spread to the Basilica in which doge Pietro Candiano IV sought shelter from the fury of the people who had risen in arms against him. He wanted to flee « *per Sancti Marci atrii ianuas* », but he was caught and slain in the church.

Outside the Basilica, on the façade towards the Piazzetta dei Leoni, there is a rather curious Byzantine-style relief, X century, representing the oriental legend of Alexander the Great's attempted ascent to Heaven: he is harnessing two mad griffins to his chariot so that they may carry him with lightning-speed to the conquest of Paradise. On the same façade, below the most westerly arch, there is a panel offering the most striking contrast to this mythical scene. It represents the *Etoimasia*, the throne of the Last Judgment below a cross which is surmounted by the Lamb, the victim of sin; on the sides, and divided into two groups, twelve sheep symbolize the Apostles, while at either end stands a palm-tree. It is a panel that speaks both to the heart and the mind. Its soberness and its eloquence make it a peerless synthesis of ideas. The palm-trees are the voice of nature and provide a concrete illustration of the Biblical text which says: '*Justus ut palma florebit*'; in their neat and disciplined arrangement the sheep are the witnesses of Christ, of which flock the Master proclaimed Himself the good shepherd. The throne, so dear to the Byzantine imagination, represents Christ-God, who alone shall judge the living and the dead. We Latins are inclined to exalt the humanity of the Saviour, the East tends to transcend the human in Him and emphasize the divine, which can be sensed but not constricted within the mortifying limits of a figurative representation. The voice of the Church has never been so eloquent as in this stone carving.

While speaking of the ornamentation on the outside of the Basilica, we must also call attention to the reliefs below the loggia on the main façade, between the arches of the doorways: two of them represent Hercules' labours, and the others the Virgin, the Angel Gabriel (recently restored), St. Demetrius and St. George, in Byzantine style.

St. Demetrius of Thessalonica and St. George — the privilege of having been his birthplace is claimed by many cities — were both martyrs, and greatly honoured and venerated in the East. In these reliefs they are shown as strong youthful warriors with fluttering chlamyses, seated on chairs and each holding a sword. They are represented like two high dignitaries of the splendid Byzantine court; placed here on the façade, at the sides of the central main arch, they keep a good watch over St. Mark's in the name of the East, whose influence is still strong.

THE PRESENT-DAY BASILICA · DOGE DOMENICO CONTARINI

A) **The Body of the Evangelist.** Tourists wandering up and down the Basilica have often asked me where St. Mark's tomb is situated. It is of course in the place of honour, under the high altar. The size of the sarcophagus is massive; today it can be seen protected by a bronze grating, through which we can read the words « *Corpus Divi Marci Evangelistae* », and at the back an inscription taken from the first epistle of St. Peter: « *salutat vos... Marcus filius meus* ». The boards of a cedar-wood chest have also been preserved, together with a parchment, on which the following words can be read: « *Hic deposita est capsa in qua ab antiquo corp. D. M. adservabatur una cum bombyce in ipsa repositum. Hac die octava mens oct. MDCCXXXV* ».

After the church of the Partecipazi was built, the venerable relics were placed in the crypt beneath the front part of the apse, in front of the Chancel, corresponding, in the present Basilica, to the section of floor covered by a huge square of Greek marble known as « the sea » because of its veining, which is reminiscent of the movement of the waves. The tomb was probably part of an actual *martiryon*, protected by screens which are certainly still extant, though put to a different use.

In ancient times the bodies of saints were not openly shown, but on the contrary ingeniously hidden lest they should be stolen. There is a legend saying that after the completion of the walls of the present Basilica people started looking for the Body of the Evangelist in order to put it in a suitable place; but Doge Pietro Orseolo the Saint had hidden it so carefully that all their searching was in wain, which caused great dismay and consternation, and public prayers and fasts were proclaimed. Then, on June 25th, 1094, when all the people were gathered in the basilica, the miracle occurred. Some stones fell from a pier, and an arm of the Saint was discov-

A longitudinal view of St. Mark's Square with the Basilica in the background.

ered. The *inventio* had taken place. The pier was the one which is standing today next to the Altar of the Sacrament. On its inner side there is a chromatic panel before which a lamp is perpetually burning in remembrance of the discovery.

A large and expressive XIII century mosaic, which can be seen in the right arm of the transept against the Altar of the Sacrament, gives the various details of the event: the whole of Venice, from the Doge to the Signoria, the Clergy, the Bishop and the People, is praying that the body may be rediscovered; then the prayer is granted and the miracle takes place. This is the comment: for three days « *plebs ieiunat — petra patet SMC collegit et collocant* ».

The altar containing the Body of the Evangelist is protected by a ciborium in dark green marble, supported by four columns in oriental alabaster decorated with reliefs representing scenes from the life of the Virgin and Christ. There is no agreement as to the date or origin of these incomparable treasures. The most widespread opinion is that they came from the East where they were carved in the V or VI century, and that they were brought to Venice from Dalmatia by Doge Pietro Orseolo II, whose exploits won him the title of Duke of Dalmatia.

St. Mark was still to speak from the tomb and the mosaics adorning the walls of the two choristers' galleries celebrate episodes from the life of the Evangelist buried beneath.

The artists understood the tie binding St. Mark to St. Peter and they show St. Mark consecrated Bishop by St. Peter, and baptizing the inhabitants of Aquileia. Then they moved on to other episodes from the Saint's life, martyrdom and burial; after centuries the Saint crosses the sea once again: he had sailed from Aquileia to Alexandria, and his Body is now brought back from Alexandria to Venice by the same route. The artist is there when the sacred relics are being carried off, he travels together with them over the treacherous sea and then shares in the exultation of Venice welcoming St. Mark as a hero.

In composition, style, colour and the ingenuous way they tell their story these mosaics are a miracle to those who can interpret them. They may be placed about the beginning of the XII century. Let us examine for a moment the mosaic representing the carrying off of the body, situated above the right singing gallery: it is the most expressive; two slender graceful columns support a lightly sketched architrave surmounted by two pinnacles; between them is visible the word « Alexandria ». A little further away an area of the mosaic is divided into three partitions by similar columns supporting an epistyle with three pinnacles; the crimson-coloured sarcophagus lies underneath. The priest Theodosius, the monk Stauracio and the two merchants, all indicated by their names, are holding the Body in their arms; Theodosius is supporting the head and the arms, Stauracio the trunk, and the Venetians the legs.

Reconstruction of the façade of the Basilica of Doge Contarini. The building is massive and yet severe in its simplicity. The decorations were added in the XV century. ▶

The solemn central doorway of the Basilica, decorated with rows of columns and the antelamic carvings of the three great arches.

The eastern side of the portico of the Basilica. A succession of very precious columns and XIII century mosaics; in the background the door to the Zen Chapel.

The creation of the world; Adam and Eve; their sin in the Garden of Eden. A splendid XII century mosaic in the first cupola to the right on entering the portico.

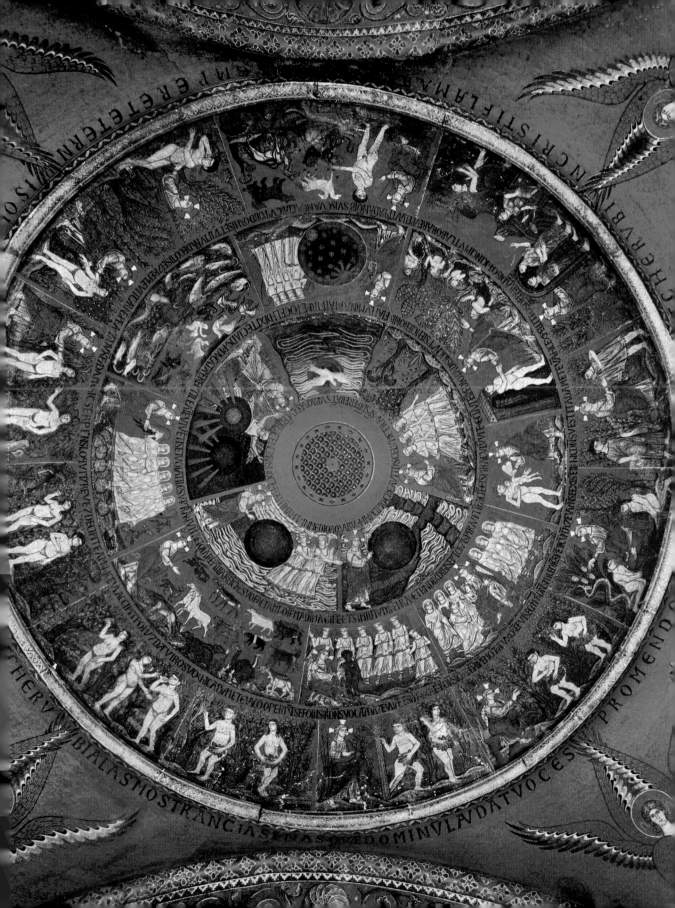

The cupola above the door of St. Clement: the mosaic decoration is the most ancient and best-preserved. The various scenes possess an ingenuous but powerful narrative quality, together with markedly realistic characteristic. The detail shows God breathing the soul into the body of Adam. Below: the introduction of man into the Garden of Eden.

Above: Adam is deeply asleep and God causes Eve to be born from his side. Below: Adam and Eve summoned to God's judgment after their sin.

Next to this there is another scene: the two Venetians have left Alexandria behind them and are hurrying off in the opposite direction with a bar on their shoulders from which hangs a big basket. Above them there is a large inscription: « *Marcus furantur kanzirii (porco) vociferantur — carnibus absconditus... fugiunt retrorsum* ». A whole drama is narrated with few strokes, and the expressions of the protagonists' faces reflect their trepidation.

The incidents that happened to St. Mark after his death are also narrated in the lunettes, arches and under-arches of the façade. In the cove of the door called « of Sant'Alipio » there is a mosaic describing the removal of the Body of the Evangelist, which is carried on the shoulders of the Prelates, accompanied by the people and welcomed by the palace dignitaries. The Saint is about to take possession of the Basilica « *ut venetos semper servet ab hostes suos* ». It is the only surviving mosaic of the cycle originally adorning the façade, which is here preserved in its most ancient representation. It is a soberly balanced mass in which movement is suggested by the way the rigid design is brought to life by splashes of colour as in an oneiric vision. The other mosaics represent the Signoria venerating the relics of the Martyr, the Clergy thronging round the Saint, and the transport of the body from Alexandria. They are mosaics from cartoons by XVII an XVIII century artists; magniloquent and pictorial, they look impressive to those who look at them from the Piazza, but they have nothing in common with the classical mosaics. The insistence on this theme was meant to proclaim out loud that « *Venetorum urbs in aquis fundata — acquarum ambitu circumsepta* » was born and lived « *divina disponente Providentia* ».

The Mosaics of the Zen Chapel have nothing to do with the Cardinal. They are contemporary with those of the narthex. They date back to the XIII century and develop the recurring theme of the life of the Evangelist: St. Mark

A view of St. Mark's Square as it probably looked in the XII century. The cupolas of the Basilica resemble those of the Pantheon. The towers of the Ducal Palace, which then looked very much like a fortress, and the campanile, which was then raised higher during the Renaissance.

Page 25 - A XIII century mosaic in the portico: Moses lets the dove fly away from the ark after the deluge.

writes the Gospel; St. Peter gives it his approval; St. Mark baptizes in Aquileia; the Dream of St. Mark in the Rialto islands; St. Mark sails for Alexandria, etc. The situation of these scenes is easily understood, since this was the place where, previous to the erection of the chapel, a great doorway opened towards the Piazzetta, serving as State Entrance for those coming from the lagoon. The first welcome to the guests had to be given by « *Missier San Marco* » who had so many stories to tell.

B) **The Structure.** St. Mark's is an extraordinary phantasmagoria, a proteiform structure out of an epic romance, a polyphony flowing from occult sources. Dawn and sunset, sunshine and mists fill it with glittering splendour or transform it with evanescent hues, and the changing patterns of light give it the quivering quality of images reflected in the rippling waters of *rii* and canals.

We owe the present Basilica to doge Domenico Contarini, who began its construction in 1063.

Domenico Contarini was a skilful politician and a brilliant soldier. Among his many successful undertakings his conquest of Grado is noteworthy, which was coveted also by the ambitious Popone, Patriarch of Aquileia.

He was on good terms with the Eastern Empire, and he too received the many pompous titles which the Court of Byzantium showered on the new men of the lagoon in order to keep them bound to its own interests. The Contarini family was one of the twelve *apostolic* families, so called for their contribution to the foundation of the city.

What were the reasons which induced Doge Contarini to take his historic decision? Venice had by now, as it were, come of age and trade had given her great wealth; she had become aware of her political and maritime strength. The Western world had been shaken to its very foundations, the East was under the threat of Turks and Normans, and Christianity itself was split into two as a result of the schism of 1054. But Venice, scarcely touched by these events, had developed into a strong state which nobody could now afford to disregard and which maintained the balance of power in the Mediterranean. This was one of the features of the age in which Contarini lived. The prestige of the Venetians was then one of the reasons which prompted him to undertake the construction of the new Basilica. The old one was too small and modest a building for the large soul of Venice and of Contarini himself, who certainly wished, deep in his heart, to hand his name down to posterity by emulating what was then being created by the cities of the Po valley.

We must not believe that the whole structure of the old building was taken to pieces and lost; some of the main walls were preserved and the ornaments, decorations and precious material were integrated into the new church.

This, however, is all we can know with certainty, and we are faced with a whole series of thorny problems. Who was the architect? Did he build upon the existing foundations? Was the original basilica plan transformed into a centralized plan, or were the previous churches already built on a centralized plan? And what changes did the Basilica undergo in those distant centuries? Many indeed are the questions which critics, architects and scholars have asked and keep asking themselves. All the contrasting theories and opinions can be equally valid, and to give an answer here to all these problems would be a foolish oversimplification.

Popular tradition identifies the architect with a relief figure at the left-hand base of the third main arch of the façade, representing a man with a cloak and with crutches between his legs, who is biting his finger in anger because of the defects and mistakes in the building, which he had promised to make perfect.

If I can express my convinction, the Basilica, though presenting original features of its own, drew its inspiration from Byzantium, and was Byzantine during its gestation; but it is not at all improbable that local masters well acquainted with their trade took part in the work; and some elements of Romanic-Lombardic art uncovered during the restorations made some decades ago indicate that the school of the Comacini masters had a hand in it, too.

Some scholars tried to establish a connection between St. Mark's and the Abbey of Pomposa, on whose façade is carved the name of a certain Maestro Mazulo, and even the monk Guittone d'Arezzo is believed to have come to Venice. But if they came at all they were no more than tourists *ante litteram.*

The architectonic structure of the Basilica rises on a plan in the form of a Greek cross, with a central nave and two aisles. The central nave leads to the Chancery and is interrupted by the transept. Powerful columns divide the nave from the aisles and the same pattern is repeated in the arms of the transept. Above the columns and round the 14 piers there are galleries or *matronei*, which run along the whole structure up to the choristers' galleries overlooking the high altar. The two aisles terminate in two little apses: in the one on the right there is the altar of St. Clement and in the one on the left the altar of St. Peter.

The Chancel, which also has an apse, is raised to allow room for the crypt beneath. The present crypt dates back to the XI century and was built by doge Vitale Falier, who was granted the special grace of the *inventio* of the Body of the Evangelist; and it is commonly believed that the relics of the Saint were preserved there from that time onward. Falier is the doge who appears in the mosaic describing the circumstances of the discovery. He is buried in a niche in the portico, decorated with mosaics and protected by various fragments of Veneto-Byzantine art. According to tradition he was not mourned when he died, since he had neglected to look after the welfare of the people.

Let us go back to the crypt. It is impossible for the visitor not to feel spell-bound at the sight of the forest of columns which fill it up completely and which are made dynamic by a succession of vaults and niches. We are struck with wonder and dismay: it is like plunging into a distant past, away from our restless time which keeps us always on the move, like the sinners in Dante's hell, « stung without pause by gadflies and wasps ».

The crypt is dimly lit by small windows opening on to the raised part of the Chancel, which is decorated by little arches and pilasters in the Byzantine style.

It was Cardinal Patriarch Angelo Giuseppe Roncalli's express wish that the tombs of the last bishops of the Venetian church should be gathered in this place and that the relics of other patriarchs, formerly preserved in various localities, should be collected here in loculi in token of gratitude and Christian piety. « The place of honour round the Body of St. Mark belongs by right to my predecessors », he used to say.

Then the dreadful disaster happened: during the flood of 1966 the water filled the crypt up to the ceiling and profaned all the tombs.

Let us enter the Basilica and look up towards the roof, at the ravishing sight of the five blind cupolas: the eighty little windows which run all along their bases produce an ecstatic effect, and the vaults, arches and spandrels complete the illusion of a dream. For the powerful structure of its aerial masses and its vast and solemn breadth, the interior of the Basilica is reminiscent of the old Roman baths. The moderate and subdued light which was needed to produce the most appropriate effect must have been supplied by windows placed in the apse and opening on to the façade or towards the south. Some of these windows have been walled up and today the Basilica receives light mainly from the large Gothic rose window situated in the end wall of the right arm of the transept and resembling a delicate piece of lacework, and from the great window against the arch of the Apocalypse which is covered in by bottle-glass panes and opens on to the terrace outside, spreading over the whole span of the main central arch. These changes took place after a fire in the XV century; up to that time the window had been protected by a delicately executed Byzantine screen with little arches and marble windows, of which some relics have been preserved.

The Basilica is encircled on three sides by a portico which was originally open toward the outside: it is divided into bays broken by exquisite little cupolas and high narrow niches which impart a plastic harmony to the whole. Its walls must have been decorated with a pictorial cycle, as is witnessed by the frescoes discovered on the left-hand wall of the Baptistry when some marble slabs were removed during recent restoration work.

The portico was not intended as a place reserved for catechumens and public penitents when service was going on inside the church, as was the case in early Christian times. If such were still the custom today, not even all the arcades which once connected Athens with the Piraeus would be sufficient to hold the black sheep denied admittance into the temple.

Originally the façade had a severe and solemn aspect. We can reconstruct it with our imagination, but the task is made easier by a drawing by A. Pellanda which reproduces it as it looked in 1100. This drawing is part of the monumental work published by Ferdinando Ongania with the collaboration of all the best minds and the most authoritative scholars at the turn of the last century.

This façade is divided, like today, into an upper and lower part by a terrace stretching its whole length and protected by a balustrade of very delicate little columns. Five great niches open in the lower part; they are crowned by a corresponding number of pointed arches in the upper part, each with a series of single or double little windows which increase the loveliness of the whole. The cupolas, like those in the Pantheon, are not visible. Such sober and sedate solemnity was well in accordance with the style of life of those days, which was still sober and disciplined.

The Basilica was built in bare brick and its reddish colour, the gravity of which was only occasionally broken by the few decorative elements, spoke a language of its own. We can still have an idea of the simple severity of the original Basilica of St. Mark of Domenico Contarini if we look up from the Piazzetta to the undecorated space between the Porta della Carta and the adjacent tower.

If instead we look at the Basilica from the top of the Campanile a completely different view spreads before us. The lead-covered roof stretches like an almost level surface from which rise, mushroom-like, the five imposing cupolas arranged in the shape of a cross. The lead covering was added to the original hemispherical structures during the XIII century. Circular bases of brick support the framework of intercrossing rafters and the whole is covered with sheets of lead variegated by time, and topped by little columns bearing false onion-shaped lanterns surmounted by decorated crosses. If we shut our eyes we feel transported into the distant East, with all its hallucinations and its dreams.

C) **The marble facings.** St. Mark's was also the Ducal Chapel, and when services were celebrated the Doge was dressed in court garments which recalled those of the great dignitaries of the Court of Byzantium.

The Basilica was the doge's home as well, it had therefore to look as imposing and dignified as the men who then held power. There was exquisite art and a real cult of the beautiful in St. Mark's, but the church had to be also a source of prestige for the rulers of a State which honoured Christ and St. Mark out of intimate conviction but also because they were its faithful allies in matters of politics.

Local and foreign visitors were struck with a sense of religious wonder at the sight of the many objects which had been gathered in St. Mark's with an ingenuousness which no doubt found encouragement in the spirit of the time. A Madonna is carved in the stone from which Moses made water spring; four columns come from Jerusalem: they belonged to Solomon's temple; behind the altar of the Baptistry there is a large mass of granite: from there Jesus spoke to the multitude. Two stones come from the prison of St. John the Baptist: they are still soaked in blood; the effigy of the Saviour which can be seen above the door of the Treasury was carved in Jerusalem while Jesus was still alive; four columns decorating the Choir belonged to the ambo from which Pilate shouted « Ecce Homo » to the people. Among so many relics there had to be something connected with St. Mark. The marble chair which St. Mark used in Alexandria and which was taken to Byzantium by the Empress Helena, Constantine's mother, and later given to the Patriarch of Grado by the Emperor Heraclius, is preserved in the treasury of the Basilica. But let us stop here and return to the regal decoration of the Basilica.

In the Chapel of St. Clement there is a fragmentary inscription of doubtful meaning, which is supposed to have been engraved in 1159 under the reign of doge Vitale Michiel and to record the beginning of the marble work on the Basilica: « coepit tabulas petrus... ». Scholars have offered controversial interpretations of this inscription; according to some « tabulas » refers to the mosaic work, according to others it refers to the marble facings. The marbles cover large sections of the walls and come from Dalmatia and the East: most of them were taken to Venice at the time of the fourth Crusade and the conquest of Constantinople (1202).

It is rather remarkable that our forefathers, who were merchants almost by natural disposition, should have cared so much to load their ships with rare and precious marbles rather than with merchandise and spices. Merchants could not have been mere vulgar money-makers, then. And we owe it to them that the walls of St. Mark's are covered with the widely differing varieties of granite, with red and white porphyry, African breccia and coralline breccia, grey and red lumachella, Parian marble and marble of Pentelicus, alabaster, jasper, agate, etc. Time has tarnished and made indistinct the colour of these marbles; but they need only be washed and all their charm is displayed once again. This is what happened recently with the wall of the left aisle. Almost in the middle of it there is a slab of « rosso veronese » marble which is now one of the compulsory sights for guides and their trains of tourists: we can discover in it the fossilized flora and fauna of prehistoric times: a parrot looks at us and cackles its welcome to all visitors. The end wall of the left arm of the transept is decorated with marble slabs opening like a book. The walls of the two aisles are covered with different varieties of marbles up to the level where the mosaics begin; the slabs of cipollin, « pavonazzetto » and Greek marble on the external wall of the Treasury make up a palette to make any painter envious.

The function of the columns is a decorative more often than an architectural one. There are five hundred of them in St. Mark's. Some are very solemn, like the six columns of Greek marble which support the matronei in the central nave; others, scattered everywhere, are of rare preciosity, like the ones decorating or supporting the ambos and the iconostasis, or the ones which are part of the little altar called « Il Capitello ». This altar preserves a Painted Crucifix which was brought here from the Piazza after blood had flowed from a wound inflicted by some sacrilegious hand. « Il Capitello » is surmounted by a globe of oriental agate.

Two orders of these columns encircle, like a forest, the three façades of the building: many run all along it above the terrace; eight porphyry columns stand at the sides of the main doorway and others stretch like a procession varying slightly, with still other similar columns scattered or grouped together in the portico. Much curiosity is aroused by two columns in one of archways on the left, on which some Armenian letters are roughly engraved. How is this to be explained? The joy of reading and conjecturing I leave to the visitor.

The two square pillars of Acre which stand in the Piazzetta in front of the south façade are very original pieces. The received opinion is that they came from San Giovanni d'Acre, as a trophy of the victory of the Venetians over the Genoese in 1256, a document of VI century Syrian art. The clusters and volutes forming the pattern of their decoration resemble similar motives that can be found on the woven materials of that area. Their monograms have been a real puzzle for scholars — by no means an unprecedented case in St. Mark's. Some believe they can read in them the following words: « To God, the Advocate and the Saviour — To God, the Supreme and the Almighty », etc. This would mean that the pillars were taken from some sacred building; maybe they supported the portico of one of the doors of the Church of San Saba.

The floor is opus sectile and opus tessellatum and dates back to the XII and XIII centuries. It is like an oriental carpet covering the whole Basilica, on which the imagination of the artists has interwoven strange and admirable designs, representing for the most part a large variety of plants and animals. One of the loveliest among them is that of a variegated little peahen which has a tuft of feathers on its red head and holds tightly in its beak a little green snake wriggling in its attempt to escape death.

With its curves and slopes the floor resembles the wavy surface of a little sea; this of course is not the work of any artist, but of time itself, in accordance with the law of irregularity which in St. Mark's seems to be a fixed rule. The complete pattern of the floor is reproduced with absolute precision in an admirable and very authoritative XVIII century design by Antonio Visentini.

D) **The mosaics.** The gold of the mosaics covers the upper part of the Basilica for more than 4,000 square metres of its surface. Hence the rather stale name of Golden Basilica. From this background emerge figures, stories, sacred and profane events.

The mosaic work can be divided into chronological cycles: the first dates back to the period from the XI century to the first half of the XIII century; the second to the XIV century; the third coincides with the Renaissance, from its beginning to the moment when it reached its height; the fourth with the centuries following.

The mosaics show a unity of conception which cannot be casual, and I accept, among the many traditions, the one of longest standing: abbot Gioacchino da Fiore, the Calabrian endowed with a prophetic spirit, dictated the theme which was then developed by the Veneto-Byzantine mosaic school.

The vaults and cupolas of the narthex are illustrated with episodes from the Bible, from « Genesis » and « Exodus »: the Creation, Adam and Eve, Noah and the Ark, the calling of Abraham, Moses and his deeds.

These protagonists of the Old Testament announce the *Homo Novus in figuris praesignatus*. Christ becomes human and divine history in the interior of the Basilica. In the cupola above the Chancel, called Cupola of the Prophets, the latter are shown with scrolls bearing inscriptions which refer to their prophecies; they cluster round the Virgin, who is, already in Eden, like the dawn of the Promise. The central cupola shows the glory of the Ascension: all is consummated and Christ ascends to Heaven in a nimbus of colours and with angels flitting all around Him. In the spandrels, under the Evangelists, there is an extraordinary group: four men pouring water from leather-bottles on their shoulders: they are the four Biblical rivers: the Tigris, the Euphrates, the Fison, and the Gylon (the Nile and the Indus). The next cupola shows the Pentecost; after receiving the Holy Ghost the Apostles preach the Gospel to the multitudes and the nations, grouped together, are waiting for the Light. The story of the Church is concluded in the Arch of the Apocalypse, and a mysterious figure hidden among the vaults of the left aisle is believed to represent the last Pope. An aureole round his head, he is, like Melchizedek, *sine nomine* and *sine genealogia*.

The mosaics of the great arch between the Ascension and the Pentecost narrate the dramatic Passion of Christ, from whose blood germinated the holy generation of the people of God. There is a comment in sober Leonine lines (rhymed or assonant hemistichs, invented by Leonius, a monk of Saint Victor in Paris, in the XII century). Unsurpassable in their sense of the divine and in their profound ingenuousness of expression, the artists still speak to us and invite us to « kneel down and pray ».

To the same cycle belong the mosaics which cover the upper part of the right aisle and represent the Prayer of Jesus in the Garden. The various figures seem lost in the wild landscape which enhances the gloom of the scene. In the great arch between the cupola of the Ascension and that of St. Leonard are represented the temptations of Christ in the desert, his triumphant entry into Jerusalem and the Last Supper. These mosaics are masterpieces of great emotional power.

The mosaics of the Baptistery and the Chapel of St. Isidore are work of the second cycle, which dates back to the XIV century. The Baptistery, which cuts short the right wing of the portico, is an alteration on the original plan of the Basilica. It contains the funeral monument of Andrea Dandolo, the doge who spent large sums for its decoration. These mosaics reflect a different style and a different temperament: the emphasis is no longer on Byzantine hieratic rigidity but on western realism: a large Crucifixion in the background and the life of the Precursor are the main themes of the composition. The mosaics above the baptismal font show an original motive: the twelve Apostles, each assisted by a deacon, immerse twelve catechumens in as many fonts; the whole is emblematic of the infancy of a new people. Four fathers and doctors of the Greek Church, Gregory Nazianzen, Basil, Athanasius and John Chrysostom, comment upon the scene with scrolls and by their facial expressions.

The mosaics decorating the little cupola above the altar are certainly the work of extremely original and imaginative artists. To the best of my knowledge this composition is unprecedented in the whole history of art. It represents Christ in glory surrounded by the nine heavenly choirs in the hierarchical order according to the theory of Pseudo-Dionysius. The angels are shown with the symbols of their power, and here lies the novelty.

The Cherubs have ten wings, the Thrones a sceptre and crown, the Dominations a rod and scales, the Principalities armour, the Seraphs a sword, etc. Angelology is very complicated. We believe angels to be manifestations of the divine power, acting as messengers between God and Man, as ministers in the work of creation, as protectors of men, communities and nations from the threats of evil.

At the foot of the altar is buried Jacopo Sansovino, the overseer of St. Mark's.

The Chapel of St. Isidore, situated at the end of the left arm of the transept, preserves the relics of the Saint of Chios, whose figure lies on a fine sarcophagus within a sort of arcosolium. The mosaics are very effective and express the true character of the Venetian school: narrative simplicity and a preference for deep tones of colour. They illustrate episodes from the Saint's troubled life, and the last scenes of the cycle describe his beheading and his arrival in Venice, which welcomes his relics with joy, for she will now have another protector in Heaven.

In the chapel there is also a baby which speaks to us from its small tomb: « *parvus eram; Phoebus mihi luxerat octo diebus* »; a bas relief at the base of a lintel warns us that the tree of life on which we are happily seated is gnawed at its roots by two moles.

The Renaissance cycle will be dealt with further on, but we can safely affirm that at the end of that period the art of mosaic died for ever. It continued as technique, and its much discussed function was mainly one of preservation and restoration; the old creative fervour had vanished into the pictorial and the dialectic.

St. Mark's has a mosaic laboratory which keeps up an age-long tradition and which, by restoring the old masterpieces, has rediscovered the secrets of the artists of the golden century.

Page 27 - A XIII century mosaic in the portico: the erection of the Tower of Babel after the deluge.

A XIII century mosaic in the portico. Above: Noah discovers wine and is unaware of its effects. Noah is drunk and Cam mocks his naked father. The two brothers Sem and Japhet cover their naked father who blesses them and curses Cam.

Below: the building of the ark: Noah takes on board two of each kind of animal for their preservation.

Together with the mosaicists I should like to mention the other trades represented in the Basilica; there are highly skilled stonemasons, carpenters, masons, joiners, smiths, and all of them feel the honour and the responsibility of working in St. Mark's. The caretakers of the church as well try to do their best, though they often have to cope with some visitor's aggressive reaction to a well-deserved criticism. Nor should we forget the people who work in the Campanile, taking care of the lift and the visitors who want to enjoy a bird's-eye view of Venice. They are also in charge of the bells and have to see that they ring at the right time, though there are cases when they decide to start ringing of their own accord, and then the city takes their sound as a warning of danger and everything is turned upside down. It is from the bells that Venice « knows tierce and none » as in the old days. They still preserve the names with which the Serenissima baptized them, according to the civic functions they performed. The sound of the *Marangona* (the largest) was a signal for the craftsmen to begin and stop work as well as a first warning for the meetings of the **Maggior Consiglio**, while the *Trottiera* reminded those who were late that they had to hurry up; the *Nona* and the *Mezza Terza* called the meetings of the Pregadi; the smallest of them, called *Ringhiera* or *Maleficio*, used to announce the capital execution of some unfortunate wretch, and people crossed themselves when they heard it.

Today the bells ring only in praise of God and as reminder for Man, who is too often absent-minded or engrossed in other preoccupations, though sometimes he can be also aggressive, if he finds that these old and discreet family voices tell him some unpleasant truth.

The Deesis (reconstruction). The great mosaic above the main door on the inside. The Virgin and Mark with the Redeemer in the middle, blessing and holding the book of life in his left hand.

The inside of the Basilica from the central nave; a superb succession of cupolas, arches and galleries. The Byzantine cross with eight arms hangs from the cupola of the Pentecost. On Solemn occasions it is up by hundred little flames. ▶

SCULPTURE AND PRECIOSITY

A) **The 'Quadriga'.** The four horses *adhinnientes and pedibus obstrepentes*, placed on the loggia against the great central arch, give plasticity and decorum to the façade of the Basilica. In their shade sat the Serenissima and its guests of honour to watch the « *feste* » and the spectacles taking place in the Piazza.

The horses were a symbol of the prestige of the Serenissima. Hence the proud boast of the Genoese admiral Pietro Doria in 1379, during the war of Chioggia: « *Signori Veneziani*, I swear by the Almighty God that we will bridle the Horses of St. Mark ». The horses were bridled for a while by Napoleon, who took them to Paris, from where they returned without the medallions of the harness. Some merciful hand took them down again during the first and second world wars for reasons of security.

They came to Venice at the time of the fourth Crusade, when they were taken from a hippodrome in Constantinople. Every Venetian considers them his own personal property, and every Venetian loves them. Their birth is wrapped in mystery. Do they come from Rome, Chios, Rhodes, Byzantium? Who can tell?

Were they cast in Greece or in Rome, and in what century? *Tot capita tot sententiae.* My personal opinion is that they are work of the Hellenistic age and were cast in the IV century. What is certain is that they have been here for eight hundred years. Their sense of lively and powerful movement, their rhythmic proportion and the loveliness of their form make these four horses of gilded bronze a unique monument and splendid sight.

Everybody nowadays has an opinion to offer: some people say that the horses are in good health, others that they are ill: the most disparate diagnoses come pouring in from all corners of the world, and suggestions concerning the therapy flood us from every side. The responsibility of the preservation of the Quadriga now lies with an international committee set up by the Ministry of Education under the aegis of UNESCO; they are studying the question and they will give their answer.

The Procuratoria of St. Mark, which has collected a whole literature on the subject, has expressed its firm opinion concerning this problem. The horses must in no case leave Venice: if necessary, they could be removed to the Marciano Museum and be replaced by perfect reproductions which should be cast in our Arsenale. The façade of St. Mark's without the Quadriga would be an insult to history and civic sense; it would be prejudicial to a long-established aesthetic exigency.

B) **The Sculptures.** Let us enter the Basilica. The iconostasis confronts us in all its majesty: the large Cross of bronze and silver in the middle and the sorrowing Virgin, St. John the Evangelist, the Apostles and St. Mark at the sides. The sculptures belong to the period of the Venetian Gothic (1394), and their great strength and vigour are the eloquent expression of the soul which created them; this work marked for Jacobello and Pierpaolo delle Masegne the culmination of their art.

Are plastic elements compatible with the interior of the Basilica? The answer ought to be a negative one. The architectonic line calls for the essential and refuses the superfluous; and yet what has been added with moderation does not offend but is in perfect harmony with the whole.

The two little altars in the apse chapels of St. Clement and St. Peter are framed by roodscreens whose architraves support statues of Saints: Magdalen, Cecilia, Christina, Catherine and Agnes: they are decorated with marble reliefs and small statues and were dear to Cristoforo Moro, the « duce serenissimo » who had them erected in 1465 and who immortalized his name with this inscription.

Cristoforo Moro was an enthusiastic admirer of St. Bernardino of Siena, to whom he was bound by deep ties of friendship. Tradition has it that St. Bernardino, who often stayed for a while at San Giobbe, prophesied he would become doge. This explains why the altar is decorated by a lovely little statue of the Saint.

On the ciborium there are six marble figures: in the front Christ between St. Mark and St. John; in the back the Redeemer between St. Mark and St. Luke, believed to be work of the XII century; the six statues in bronzed terracotta above the Canons' Choir are attributed to Pietro da Salò, who moulded them in the XVI century. Another noteworthy group of statues in Venetian-Romanic style is preserved in the Zen Chapel; of particular interest are the two pillar-bearing lions, previously used, it is said, to decorate the main door, and the relief carving of an Angel with the globe bearing a cross, supposedly dating back to the late Roman Empire. The Baptistry is decorated with an expressive group representing La Pietà and with XIV century reliefs with the Baptism of Christ, the Angel, Our Lady of the Annunciation and other sacred themes. In the pilasters of the Chancel there are two Gothic tabernacles (XIV century), decorated inside with lovely niches with figures in full relief. They served as repositories for relics and holy oil. A few years ago some light-fingered hand made away with a little statue, which now certainly enriches some foreign collection or museum.

An eagle and an incensing angel, of Byzantine inspiration, decorate the superb left ambo; from its enclosed plat-

The ambo on the left of
the iconostasis: its very
fine architecture is of
Moorish inspiration. It
can be reached through
a staircase on the side.
The Bible was read from
the lower tier and the
Gospel from the upper.
The marbles and the
carvings make this jewel
even more precious.

form springs up a Moorish oriental structure with a little cupola supported by slender little columns, a place fit for the liturgy of the Word on great occasions.

There are also many details which usually escape the eye of a hasty visitor, like the little cornices and pilasters, the hanging arches, lintels, tori, paterae, dentils, plutei and screens scattered everywhere, decorating the architectonic structure.

I once met a distinguished-looking gentleman from France who wanted to study what he considered to be the most interesting things in the Basilica. What were they? The capitals of the columns. As with the angels, each capital is different from all others. There is variety enough to satisfy every taste; there are Byzantine capitals, Romanic ones, capitals shaped like baskets, truncated pyramids or cones; many are decorated with arabesque and floral motives; in some the carving is very light, in other the pattern stands out in high relief. Particularly fine are the gilded capitals with goats' heads peeping out at the sides, which crown the six columns of the central nave, and the ten Corinthian capitals arranged in twos against the piers of the side aisles.

Four gilded angels rest solidly on ledges placed in the upper part of the corners of the piers supporting the central cupola. They are a source of great delight for the spirit. They were born in the XIII century but will live through eternity. Each of them has a language of its own: they play, sing, speak or perform a rite with an expression of heroic strength quite in keeping with their rank of high dignitaries of the celestial court. The angel above the right ambo is blowing a *shofar* (horn) with all its might, like the Hebraic priest, and yet he seems to be playing like a child.

C) **The Doors.** Let us go out and pause in front the doors. St. Mark's is also called the Basilica with the eleven bronze doors: they too have a history. The central door and the door of St. Clement are Byzantine work executed under the Emperor Alessandro Comneno. The door of St. Clement has 28 panels, deorated with inlaid gold wire and various designs with Greek inscriptions celebrating various figures of fathers and doctors of the Oriental Church. The decorations of the main door, which seems to be of local workmanship of a later period though still with traces of Byzantine inspiration, are less mannered but more effective. This door has 48 panels, 36 of which decorated with statuesque and realistic figures covered with enamel; several of the saints are Latin: Ermagora, Fortunato, Tecla and Cecilia. The work was executed for Leo da Molino, « worshipful procurator », who is shown kneeling down before St. Mark; the date is about 1112. The door was recently washed and restored, and has now regained its old charm and original splendour.

The main door opening on to the Piazza has a background of bronze plating; its cornices, cord designs, rosettes and heads of animals are later additions; the date of its execution is lost in the mists of time. The bronze doors with cruciform designs and grills are of classical inspiration; they bear the signature of *magister Bertucius aurifex veneratus* and the date 1300.

D) **The Antelamic Sculpture.** The central doorway consists of three great arches whose inner and outer fascias are decorated with reliefs. Once coloured with gold and blue, these reliefs show the evolution of the art of sculpture from the plastic quality of the Romanic period to the more expert craftsmanship of the Lombard masters and then to the first cadences of the Gothic. The first arch celebrates the triumph of wild nature, yet untamed by man. The reliefs of the second arch represent the months of the year, each of them illustrated with the labour attached to it in rural life: in February an old man warms himself by the fire, in June a peasant reaps the corn, etc. The arch is also decorated with figures emblematic of the virtues. The reliefs of the third arch show easily identifiable arts and trades. This unity of conception is a hymn to work sung by the society of the XIV century, by then full of confidence in its destiny, for the free Commune had favoured the development of the personality and self-awareness of its industrious people. The seed sown by Benedetto Antelami had by then sprouted also in St. Mark's, which is decorated with vigorous reliefs also in the upper part of its façade.

From the age of the people we then go back to an age of kings and courts: we refer to the porphyry head so called of « the dead man » or « Il Carmagnola » situated at the east corner of the balustrade; it is of Syrian origin and is supposed to be a portrait of the Byzantine Emperor Justinian II « of the broken nose ». The porphyry group so called « of the thieves » which stands next to the Porta della Carta, at the corner of the square building in the shape of a tower where the Treasure is kept, has similar characteristics. Popular tradition identifies them with four thieves trying to steal the Treasure of St. Mark. In reality these figures (the Moors) are those of the wielders of power on earth, the four Emperors of the late Roman Empire, embracing one another to seal a pact which must have certainly streamed with blood. It seems to me that the popular nickname of thieves is most appropriate.

E) **The Treasure.** It is the richest of its kind in the world; it is now collected into three rooms which for centu-

Angel playing. It is one of the four powerful Romanesque sculptures situated in the upper part of the corners of the pillars on which the central cupola rests. They may be said to act like a chorus to the events represented in the mosaic of the cupola: the Saviour ascends to Heaven seated on the variegated rainbow while angels are about him in many-coloured splendour. It is an apocalyptic vision.

ries have undergone alterations and adaptations. The Republic used them as a repository for relics, trophies taken from every part of the world and precious objects pawned by kings and princes. The technique of *Rififi* was evidently well known also in those centuries. In 1249 Canditotto Stamatti dug an underground passage and robbed « the ark of God »; in 1797 the Municipality had less trouble and more luck: four men and four women perpetrated the sacrilege at San Galliano, by order of the authorities and by means of a stove: many of the rarest pieces were melted to obtain bars of gold and silver and precious stones; a whole patrimony of history and art, which had been collected during ten centuries, was dispersed; quite a few objects, however, were missed by the jackals.

The room called the Sanctuary holds a little altar with a frontal of oriental alabaster, and sixteen niches containing 110 reliquaries. There are relics of the Passion: fragments of the Cross, one of the nails which transfixed the Lord, a fragment of the flagellation column, a shred of the purple robe with which Christ was covered in mockery, etc. The rarest piece is the relic of the Precious Blood, which Enrico Dandolo brought from Constantinople in 1202. The reliquaries are specimens of the unsurpassable art of the Byzantine and Venetian goldsmiths; they are also associated with the names of Greek emperors and empresses.

Let us pause for a moment before the reliquary of the Empress Irene Dukas, wife of Alessio I Comneno. It contains fragments of the Sacred Wood arranged in the shape of a cross; it is a Byzantine piece of the beginning of the XIII century, decorated with a silver gilt. Irene, who became a nun in 1118, had a Greek dedicatory inscription engraved in it: « ...I, Irene, Empress of the House of Dukas, servant of God, once clad in gold, now clad in sackcloth, once clad in linen, now in rags, the Empress who preferred sackcloth to purple... ».

Apart from those of the Passion, the Sanctuary is full of the most strange relics of apostles, martyrs, saints, men and women *quas numerare nemo poterat*. The skull of St. Titus, first bishop of the Christian community of Crete, was, for instance, only recently restored to that church in the spirit of the Oecumenic Council. Why so much love for relics? And what caused this ardent longing to possess them? Christian piety, certainly, and maybe a tinge of fetishism; but people were convinced that to possess the relic meant to oblige the saint to act as a *numen loci tutator*.

The Treasury proper, whose walls are more than one metre thick, contains many chalices in hard stone, book covers chased in high relief and decorated with enamels, candelabra, altar-frontals, icons, and profane objects. All the countries of the East are represented here, even China. Marco Polo is supposed to have enriched the collection with the precious objects he brought back from his fabulous journey.

A small reliquary box of silver gilt decorated with the lilies of France deserves special mention; it belonged to Charles VIII, king of France, and fell into the hands of the Venetians in the battle of Fornovo.

An exquisitely wrought Persian turquoise bowl with an Arabic inscription (X century) was sent to Venice as a gift by the Shah Azum Hassa in the XV century. The Fatimite Caliph Aziz Billach is represented by a rock crystal vase for water of the X century; the vase bears an inscription in Cufic characters and the decoration is original. This object is much though of in Egypt, and it is little wonder that they borrowed it for an exhibition which was held at Cairo some years ago.

The Marciano Museum, which has recently been housed in the rooms above the wings of the portico, in the complement of the Treasury. It contains precious lace of the Venetian school which conquered Europe. The members of the aristocratic world of the courts used to vie with one another in displaying these refined adornments, whose fashion had been started by the dogaresse. It is little wonder therefore that, at the turn of the last century, Margherita of Savoia, first Queen of Italy, became the patroness of the Burano lace school, whose *mistra* (mistress) was Cencia Scarparola; she alone had kept the secret and the skill of the *punto buranese* (Burano stitch).

Among the most valuable pieces of the Marciano Museum there are gradual books and antiphonaries, medieval and Renaissance tapestries, four tapestries with scenes of the Passion, the tapestries called « of the Emperor » and those called « of St. Mark », Persian carpets and paintings, fragments of ancient mosaics, the double-bass of Gaspare da Salò, and the great XVI century ducal throne, of wood with carvings, which the doge used during ceremonies in St. Mark's.

F) **The Gold Altar Screen.** On the eve of the Festa del Redentore there is in Venice a firework display culminating with the « *rocheton* » (big rocket); for quite a time the sky is shaken by a storm of thunder-claps and lit up by myriads of flashes of colour. The effect produced by the gold altar screen is not dissimilar. This piece too has an adventurous history. It was first ordered in Constantinople and then went through the hands of various doges, from Pietro Orseolo to Ordelafo Falier, to Pietro Ziani, to Andrea Dandolo. This means that the original altar-screen underwent a long process of alteration and enlargement, being all that time considerably added to and embellished. Giovanni Boninsegna was the last artist who worked at it. In 1342 he put his signature on the wood in which the plates are inset: « ...me fecit - orate pro me ».

The words « me fecit » require an explanation: Boninsegna only remodelled the piece, altering the previous arrangement and setting the enamels, which seem to have come from the Pantocrator monastery in Constantinople. The central panel represents Christ blessing surrounded by the Evangelists; in the upper part of the screen the holy-days of obligation of the liturgy; saints, prophets and angels are scattered in symmetrical order against the vast background. The Virgin is shown between the Empress Irene and the Emperor Alessandro Comneno, here transformed to represent Doge Ordelafo Falier. There is gold in profusion and the workmanship of the goldsmiths is superb. I must mention, for the sake of curiosity, that the altar-screen numbers 1300 pearls, 400 garnets, 90 amethysts, 300 sapphires, 300 emeralds, 15 rubies, 75 balas-rubies, 4 topazes, and 2 cameos. How did the masterpiece survive the wickedness of men and the times? The descendants of the old Venetian merchants must evidently have still possessed some of the cunning of their forefathers; they could take advantage of the ignorance of thieves but were also, of course, helped by their good luck.

The most distinguished authorities in this field came to Venice from all over the world under the auspices of the Giorgio Cini Foundation, and by its founder's express wish, in order to study the Gold Altar Screen and the Treasure. The work of so many experts, critics and scholars lasted for years and their discoveries and conclusions were collected into two volumes recently published by Sansoni in a sumptuous edition.

The last word was said on the Gold Altar Screen and the Treasure; gaps were filled, and problems and questions

The iconostasis. A Gothic XV century structure. The Apostles and the Saints on the side of the monumental cross dominating the interior of the Basilica were carved by the Dalle Masegnes. The columns and the marbles are exceptionally precious. The whole structure is reminiscent of the Byzantine iconostasis.

were faced and scientifically solved. The world of art and culture scored a success for Venice and the civilization which has in the Island of San Giorgio a meeting-point of the many ways which are open to the spirit of free men.

The Gold Altar Screen and its central panel. This masterpiece of goldsmithry was begun in the X century and executed partly in Byzantium and partly in Venice. During the following three centuries it underwent many additions and alterations in accordance with the function it was destined to perform.

THE RENAISSANCE

The anonymous author of a minor chronicle writes: « in 1415 the figures were made and higher up the flowers, and stone leaves began to be placed round the arches.». St. Mark's felt the air of the new spring, and the « decorated Gothic » which triumphed in Venice during the early Renaissance transformed the twelve external arches into ogives and grafted the luxuriant rampant vegetation onto the façade. From this wood emerge statues and gargoyles, and saints stand out with half their figures, and other saints rise aloft on the pinnacles, and more saints enter the kiosks between the arches, leaving the place of honour to St. Mark surrounded by a host of flying angels.

The winged lion stands out in the central arch against a blue and starry background; by then it held sway over the skies of the Adriatics, the Mediterranean and the provinces of the Italian mainland. Fortitude and Justice, the civic virtues, crown the pinnacles to the south and make up, together with the rest of the façade, a glorious view for those coming from the sea. The Venetian *taiapiera* worked together with stonemasons from Tuscany and Lombardy, who were destined to leave profound and lasting traces in our city. Their art contributed to the waning of our old sensibility and the rise of new conceptions in the fields of the sculptural and architectural arts. Towards the end of the XV century the crowning of the façade was *perfecto* (completed). A large painting by Gentile Bellini, « The Procession of the Cross in the Piazza San Marco », reproduces a façade which was going to remain unaltered for the following five centuries.

And did the structure of the Basilica suffer any change? I should say not, unless we want to consider the two corner arcades added in the XII century, which widened the prospect of the façade, and the *matronei* which once covered also the side aisles.

Under the *matronei* of the central nave there are two inscriptions which run along their whole length. The one on the right reads: *Historiis. Auro. Forma. Specie. Tabularum. Hoc. Templum. Marci. Fore. Dic. Decus. Ecclesiaru.*

The north façade of the Basilica with the kiosk and the flowery decorations added during the Renaissance.

The little altars of St. Paul and St. James against the pillars of the transept are two jewels of Lombard art erected in the XVI century. In the east transept, within solemn arches supported by oriental columns surmounted by gilded Corinthian capitals, stand the Altar of the Sacrament covered by a Ciborium (on the right) and the Altar of the Nicopeia (on the left). They were erected in the XVII century. Above: the little altar of St. Paul and the altar of the Nicopeia. Below: the little altar of St. James and the Altar of the Sacrament.

The south façade of the Basilica, altered in the XVI century. On the side, a part of the tower-shaped building where the treasure of St. Mark is now kept. At the basis of the building there are four porphyry statues, representing the tetrarchs sealing their alliance with an embrace.

A XIII century mosaic in the vault of the left Choir; the body of the Evangelist is brought to our lagoon.

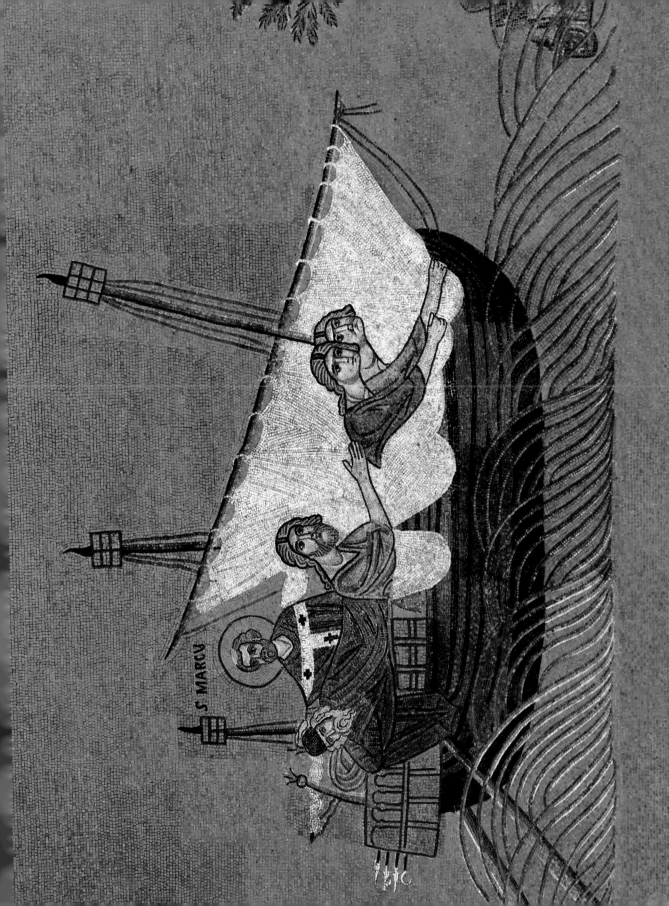

One thinks of Michelangelo throwing his hammer against the knee of his Moses. The inscription on the left reads: *Intra. Dimitte. Post. Offer. Des. Rogitato. Aulam. Peccanti. Domino. Miseris. Miserentem.* It is an appeal to God to be infinitely merciful on those penitents who used to assemble here and who were obliged to leave the church when a certain part of the service was to be performed.

The Renaissance created two jewels inside the Basilica: the little altars of St. Paul and St. James, exquisite work by Lombard masters, erected under doge Cristoforo Moro and situated against the pilasters of the transept.

Under the reign of doge Francesco Foscari St. Mark's was added a new chapel, called « Madonna dei Mascoli » (of the Males) because it belonged to a confraternity whose members were all misogynists. The marble decorations are superb. The altar, an example of the decorated Venetian-Gothic, is ornamented with statues by Bartolomeo Bon and a frontal with the relief figures of two angels bearing censers. The mosaics of the vault narrate scenes from the life of the Virgin: the old patterns have been forsaken and the naturalism of the Renaissance predominates. The cycle is the work of a Venetian, Michele Giambono; but he was certainly assisted by the great masters of Paduan and Tuscan painting (Mantegna and Andrea del Castagno).

The evolution of the art of mosaic culminates in the grandiose pictorial cycle of the vault and lunettes of the sacresty, which marks also the climax of the ornamental tendency. The figures are taken from cartoons by the great painters of the XVI century and were executed by mosaicists of good distinction, to whom we owe also the four lunettes in the upper part of the façade, celebrating the Deposition from the Cross, the Descent into Limbo, the Resurrection and the Ascension. To this celebration of the Church Triumphant corresponds, in the lower part, the exaltation of the Venetian Church with the sumptuous iconography of the adventurous vicissitudes of the Body of the Evangelist.

Since we mentioned the sacresty it would be interesting to know that some of the rooms in which the sacred vestments and utensils are now stored were once the seat of the Tribunal of the Inquisition, and that others were used as cells for its unfortunate victims. This fact, perpetuated by the names these rooms have preserved up to the present day, seems very strange. Why did the Holy Office decide on this rather singular place as its seat? The precincts were sacred and belonged by right to the Church. At the same time, however, they were under the jurisdiction of the State, which was therefore entitled to have the last word. The ecclesiastical policy of Venice suffered no prejudice; diplomacy had really become an art and a science in the XVI century.

The Zen Chapel, in the right corner of the portico, is also an expression of the Renaissance (early XVI century). Cardinal Zen, nephew of the Venetian Pope Paul II, wished a funeral chapel to be erected in St. Mark as an acknowledgment of his merits. The Republic consented only in part, for Cardinal Giambattista Zen was relegated outside the church. Almost all the decorations are manneristic and weak. The object of greatest curiosity is the gold-tipped shoe which the Virgin gave to a beggar who had offered her his most valuable possession, that is, a shoe. The whole construction is cumbersome and plethoric, and the church would have gained considerably if the corner of the portico had been left unobstructed so as to give room and light to the solemn movement of the simple architectonic structure. Jacopo Sansovino, to whom we owe the four bronze statues of the loggia, the purest and most chaste example of Renaissance sculpture, must certainly have been unpleasantly surprised at the sight of the chapel.

Sansovino came to Venice after the sack of Rome (1527) and was appointed overseer of the Basilica by the Procurators of St. Mark. The church was threatened by dangerous cracks and fissures, and the architect built the two robust abutments against the external wall of the apse. Sansovino carved the reliefs decorating the balustrades of the choristers', galleries overlooking the Chancel, and his are also the four little statues of the Evangelists on the balustrade of the Chorus, the little door of the tabernacle against the apse, and the bronze door leading from the Chancel to the sacresty, inspired, in its general structure, by the doors of the Baptistry in Florence by Ghiberti. Among the decorations of the door there are portraits of Titian, Aretino, Palladio, Veronese and Sansovino himself, immortalized by his own superb art. Sansovino was a great artist for originality and sense of composition, for the immediacy with which he captured and reproduced nature, and for the deep humanity pervading both his single figures and his choral masses.

Great sensation was caused at that time by what can be called the trial of the century. A charge of fraud was brought against Francesco and Valerio Zuccato, mosaicists of St. Mark's: instead of using genuine tesserae and coloured enamels they had retouched and shaded off their compositions by means of « the brush ». Titian, Sansovino, Tintoretto and Veronese had to appear as witnesses and experts. The verdict was as follows: « the court has decided that this was not well done; the defendants shall do the work again in a manner befitting its character and at their own expense ». What can we say about it? Evidently the beast with the pointed tail is a species which can be met with in all ages.

The whole surface of the floor of the Basilica is covered by an immense mosaic. The most interesting is the mosaic covering the floor of the right wing of the transept, which looks like an oriental carpet with its rich pattern and great variety of colours. It contains grotesque scenes of animals and fables.

Above: a peahen holding a snake in her beak. She is a symbol of immortality and the snake is a symbol of evil. The mosaic can be seen in front of the Altar of the Sacrament.

Below: a bird of prey fighting with a wild beast.

THE VIRGIN IN ST. MARK'S

I have tried to count the iconographies of the Virgin which unfold themselves in St. Mark's; they are more than forty, an incontrovertible evidence of how appealing the cult of Mary was to our ancestors and to the old artists. Mary is repeatedly portrayed in the façades; like a queen she crowns the door leading to the left transept and, on the inside, the central main door; she welcomes you when you cross the threshold of the Chapels of St. Clement and St. Peter; *Mater Ecclesiae*, she is shown in all her splendour in the cupolas, surrounded by hosts of athletic angels; she looks at you from countless pilasters, where she appears with the most strange names: « of the Kiss, of the Gun, of the Graces, of the Consolation »; she is represented in the columns of the ciborium; the Chapel of the Mascoli is devoted to her, and the litany could go on.

May I mention my personal preferences? Above the right ambo there is a little statue of the Virgin leaning to one side to support the child she is contemplating with much tenderness, and this sight thrills me with delight. I am reminded of Jacopo della Quercia. I find very moving also the little figure of the Virgin which peeps shyly and discreetly out of a niche in the central doorway. In the cove outside Mary is in glory with her triumphant Son; here she seems to want to escape the visitor's attention, which must instead be concentrated all on the focal point, the majestic figure of St. Mark, who, ravished with delight and clad in sumptuous garments, occupies the great cove, and is surmounted by a little hand with three stretched fingers coming out from among the clouds as evidence of predestination (Titian or Lorenzo Lotto?). Curiosity is still aroused by the praying Virgin in the upper lunette of the façade towards the Piazzetta; two lamps are lit every night on either side of the image in memory, as tradition has it, of the « poor Fornaretto » who was executed by mistake.

The mystery of the Annunciation is a motive which recurs very often in the decorations of St. Mark's and we already know why. It appears in the fantastic crown of the façade, in the two little statues of the altar known as « Il Capitello », on the wall of the arcosolium in the Chapel of St. Isidore, in the enamels of the Gold Altar Screen, and in two vigorous XV century statues preserved in the Treasury. The Angel kneels with spread wings before Mary who looks surprised but also serene and composed, and I am reminded, by association, of the Rialto bridge. This monuments is, for better or for worse, the true emblem of the city. Our forefathers wanted the mystery of the Annunciation to be celebrated here as well, in full sight and in high relief. The figures of the Angel and the Virgin can be seen on either side of the bridge, while from the pediment the dove directs its heavenly rays upon Mary: « *Spiritus Sanctus superveniet in te* ».

The two little statues of the Virgin and the Angel now preserved in the Treasury used once to stand in full view on two high columns under the ciborium of the high altar, a situation by which their effect was greatly enhanced. The ciborium was then covered by a cupola of gilt wood.

We shall now consider the Virgin Nicopeia, the protectress of Venice. It could hardly be otherwise, since it was St. Luke who portayed her venerable features. This panel came from a monastery in Constantinople in the XIII century, and tradition has it that it was carried at the head of the imperial armies since it was, as the name itself indicates, Nicopeia, that is, literally, « maker of victory ». It represents the Virgin with the child and it is kept in a double frame, one of which of great value for the gold and the enamels of the decoration; the Venetians venerated the Nicopeia for centuries, decorating it with gifts, votive offerings and all they had of most precious and dear. The image was very jealously preserved, and it was shown to the people only on very solemn occasions; in the XVII century it was definitively placed on the present altar, whose architecture repeats that of the altar of the Sacrament.

Whole generations have knelt and still kneel in front of this image, in hope, in invocation and in prayer; the people and the authorities came here to find comfort when the times were sad and to rejoyce in the hour of joy. Cardinal Patriarch La Fontaine hung here the war-cross which the Supreme Military Command had rightly conferred on him in 1918.

In St. Mark's there is a complete, though discontinuous, figurative cycle on the Virgin. The mosaics of the right arm of the transept show the priest Issachar mortifying Joachim and Anna because of the sterility of their marriage. The Angel comforts the old God-fearing couple with a promise that a child will be born to them; Isaiah, the prophet who had said « *Ecce virgo concipiet* », confirms the Angel's prophecy; the predestined child is born and presented in the temple. The narration continues on the wall opposite the altar of the Nicopeia, covered with mosaics of the golden period. The events refer to the infancy of Mary and are taken from the *Protoevangelium Jacobi*. The various scenes represent the life of the Virgin in the temple where she had been consecrated; the Virgin receiving the cloth to prepare the veil for the Temple; her marriage with Joseph, the fortunate suitor, whose stick only had flowered among many; the Annunciation, which takes place in a way different from that described by St. Luke, etc. The relief of the Nativity framed by the Arab-Moorish arch above the Flower Doorway is reminiscent of *I Fioretti di San Francesco*.

In the scenes of the Redemption in the cupolas and the great central arch on which they rest Mary appears with unconspicuous modesty. The mosaics in the Chapel of the Mascoli represent the last moments of the All Holy: the *dormitio Virginis*, which ends the sacred and human drama of a singular life.

At the close of solemn feast-days the people in prayer follow the Patriarch and the Clergy who go in slow procession and chanting litanies to pay honour to the Nicopeia. Cardinal Patriarch Angelo Giuseppe Roncalli said that this custom is extremely original and sublimely lyrical.

Page 47 - The Virgin Nicopeia after the recent restoration. She is considered the protectress of Venice. Her image is set in a wonderful frame where hard stones alternate with enamels with figures of Saints and Prophets.

◀ The Virgin in prayer. A very expressive XIII century mosaic. The figure of Mary is reminiscent of the Madonnas in the cove of the apse at Torcello and in that of San Donato at Murano.

YESTERDAY AND TODAY

The Basilica became the Cathedral of the Diocese at the beginning of the last century. Up to then the title had belonged to the Church of San Pietro di Castello; after the Patriarch left, his residence was abandoned and became property of the State, which employed it for military and civil purposes. This fact was much regretted by Patriarch Roncalli, who would have liked to buy the building back and destine it to some social function in accordance with the times; he also meant to collect into some of the rooms the relics of the first Patriarch, Saint Lorenzo Giustiniani, who had holily ended his days in that place. The business was already fairly under way, but then the Curia had to drop it because of more pressing pastoral cares on the mainland.

Patriarch Roncalli had more success with the redemption of the island of San Giorgio in Alga, which had also become property of the State. As a matter of fact the idea of buying it back had already been considered in 1947, the centenary of St. Benedict's death, but then nothing was done because of the exorbitant price asked by the holder of the commission and also because the Camaldolensians, who had been urged to take possession of the island, were obliged to decline the invitation on account of the practical difficulties they would have met in founding a monastery on that site.

The island is very dear to the Venetians because St. Lorenzo Giustiniani is present there and because it was once, during the XV century, an oasis of deep spirituality, the centre of a movement of reformation, *in capite et in membris*, of the Church, then floundering in a painful and tormented moral crisis.

Patriarch Roncalli redeemed the island, which is now property of the Patriarchal Seminary. The fact is full of moral and historical significance, since San Giorgio in Alga seems to be the victim of a malignant fate. To what use can it be turned? Subject as it is to continuous erosion, without a proper landing-stage and with no drinking water or electric current, only a heroic will and a heroic imagination will be able to bring it back to livable conditions.

The fall of the Serenissima marked the end of the glorious secular function of the Basilica. No more popular assemblies, or ducal trains, or aulic ceremonials; ensigns were no longer entrusted to the « *grandi capitani de mar* », or solemn oaths sworn on the Tomb of the Evangelist, or doges presented to the people from the ambo of porphyry and jasper with the ritual formula « *questo xe el vostro doge, se el ve piase* » (this is your doge, if you like him), which was followed by the *acclamatio*; no longer did potentates enter the Basilica in triumph to pay honour to St. Mark and thereby homage to the power and splendour of the Republic. All that was turned to dust.

But St. Mark's remained: the old ceremonials had been succeeded by the solemn rites performed according to the Roman pontifical and from that time onward our Patriarchs have been passing under the majestic vaults to celebrate the divine mysteries. I can still see the hieratic and ascetic Cardinal Pietro La Fontaine advance through two wings of people reaching out their hands to touch him and cross themselves. He was considered a saint and when he spoke from the pulpit it was with such evangelic simplicity, and always with quotations from Dante, for to him the *Divine Comedy* was the fifth Gospel, that nobody could resist the profound fascination he unconsciously exercised. And I can still see also Cardinal Piazza, with his statuesque figure and majestic carriage, and hear the deeply affecting modulations of his masculine voice when he sang the Preface and the *Pater Noster* according to the Gregorian variations which imparted so much emotion to the prayer. In the glitter of the purple were reflected centuries of luminous history.

Too much magnificence? How many people will be converted in Jerusalem by the mortifying bareness imposed on all rituals by the mysticism of the iconoclasts? Of the latter Herostratus was the precursor.

The Basilica was for centuries the Doge's Chapel; he used to take part in the rites together with the Signoria, like Charlemagne in St. Peter's on the famous Christmas night, or King Ruggero in the Cathedral of Monreale. From 1252 to 1772 the doges used to hang their escutcheons in St. Mark's. They were all taken down « because of the very serious damage caused to the sacred walls by the weight of the escutcheons... and in order to enhance the magnificence and the sumptuosity of such a precious monument ». When a doge died the funeral train used to pause before the main door of the Basilica, where the bier was solemnly lifted up nine times in token of public honour. In the Basilica the doge sat on a royal chair next to the altar, often, in the last centuries, with the dogaressa by his side. The Chancel was sometimes hung with tapestries and precious cloth which prevented the spectators from enjoying the fascination of the scene and filled the whole with the arcane quality of a Byzantine ceremony.

When out of the Palace the doge was accompanied by his court, whose number and sumptuous attire varied according to a rigid ceremonial. On his head he wore a very original and curious cap, called « *corno* » (horn); it derived from the seamen's pilei, which in their own turn were modelled on the classical pilei of the Dioscuri. It changed shape many times, till in the XIV century it took on the final one, consecrated by various famous paintings. Its preciosity and decoration varied, and several specimens were preserved in the Treasury till they were destroyed in the storm of 1797. One can still be seen in the Correr Museum; it is made of gold brocade, with a close-fitting coif and flaps over the ears, probably as a protection of the « zoia » (the precious cap). The standard model is reproduced in Gentile Bellini's portrait of doge Giovanni Mocenigo.

The doge, poor thing, had to come down into the Basilica more than thirty times a year; if to these we add the official and votive visits to monasteries and churches in the city, it is obvious that his function, in the life of the Republic, was mainly a representative one. The Venetian Pope Paul II, faced with the claims of the Cardinals' College to limit and control the power of the « Somme Chiavi » (St. Peter's Keys), used to answer that « he did not want to be reduced to the weak position of a doge continually watched by juntas of noblemen ».

Since we are speaking of churches I should like to call attention on a rather singular fact. As far as I know, no other town has, like Venice, so many churches dedicated to prophets of the Old Testament: Moses, Jeremiah, Samuel, Job, etc. I have asked some liturgists, but nobody has been able to tell me the reason.

The doge exercised in the Basilica the authority of a bishop; he received the holy water, incense, kisses of peace and genuflections of honour, and it seems that on certain occasions he also gave blessings. He appointed the officiating priests and they were under his jurisdiction.

The Pope accepted this state of things and a shower of Golden Roses from the Tiber seemed to sanction it, and if some Patriarch wanted to interfere with the matter he always had the worst of it, for conventions, traditions and privileges of long standing were enough to reduce him to silence. The doge could proclaim at any time that he was « solus dominus patronus et unus gubernator Ecclesiae D. Marci ». St. Mark's was in the doge's heart of hearts. The best evidence of this is the desire expressed by doge Francesco Erizzo, who died in 1645, that his heart should be put into a jasper urn and buried under the floor on the left of the high altar. The place is marked by a small marble slab with a decoration in the shape of a doge's cap.

The Procurators of St. Mark are a magistrature which dates back at least to the age of the Orseoli, and whose number and prestige increased greatly during the centuries. They were in charge of the sound administration of the Basilica, of its preservation, restoration, decoration and ornamentation. « They were always wearing a toga, since theirs was one of the highest offices of the Republic ». Some of them, however, got into trouble, either because of their negligence or because they found fault with the time-worn fabric of the State. Giorgio Pisani, who was appointed Procurator in 1780, was arrested the day after his triumphal nomination and sent to the castle of San Felice at Verona. He was a hot-head, yet his ideas were not democratic: his aim was to bring about the restoration of the old aristocratic Republic, which had by then turned into an oligarchical state.

The Procuratoria di San Marco was set up again by Royal Decree on July 9, 1931.

This historical name was chosen because it expressed better than any other the prestige attached to the functions of those in charge of the integral preservation of the Basilica and the inestimable art treasures it contains. Today it is the Patriarch who is the « solus Dominus et unus gubernator » of St. Mark's; matters of cult are attended to by the Metropolitan Chapter. The functions of the Procuratoria, even if limited by the times and the scarcity of means, are still, by decree of the « Dominus et gubernator », the traditional ones. The Procurators have to deal with the State and the various boards for the protection of the art patrimony, administer the scanty funds and look after the preservation and consolidation of a monument which obviously feels both its age and the hostility of the times and is in need of urgent, continuous and difficult repairs. These works fall under the care of the « Proto », an expert appointed by the Procuratoria, with whose approval he then takes all the measures suggested by his science, experience and love for St. Mark's. The names of many who were called to this high office are indissolubly linked with the history of the Basilica, both for their doctrine and their sometimes daring but always responsible and intelligent work.

The rather numerous Palatine Clergy of St. Mark's had several functions. Their acknowledged moderator was the Primicerius a high dignitary who enjoyed great honour and many privileges; in our opinion, however, and be it said without disrespect, he was only the first chaplain of the doge: « let the Primicerius govern the spiritual affairs of the church, but only in compliance with the orders of the doge ». In the XV century the Primicerius and the rest of the clergy took up their residence at Sant'Apollonia, after the Benedictines from Ammiana had given the Monastery to the Doge's Chapel.

At the beginning of the XVIII century the election of Pietro Barbarigo to the dignity of Primicerius was facilitated by an auspicious event: a dove entered the assembly room and alighted on the shoulder of Senator Gerolamo, who was Pietro's father: it was a manifest indication. With Luigi Paolo Foscari the long series of the Primiceri came to a triumphant end for Foscari was raised to the patriarchate; he was a very pious man, and when he died he left behind as a blessing the memory of the luminous virtues of which he was a pattern.

The precincts of Sant'Apollonia, which had been property of the State since 1807, were bought back by the Procuratoria di San Marco in 1964, after fifteen years of burocratic complications. It was then no more than a dilapidated ruin, but after its restoration its unique rather than rare little cloister of the XIII century became again one of the architectural jewels of Venice and St. Mark's. It contains the collection of stones and reliefs from the Basilica as well as the Marciana Chapel, whose achievements in the field of music won it much distinction. There is also a mosaic school which has reached excellent standards in a very short time and is now more and more thought of both in Italy and abroad. The building is also destined to receive the Diocesan Museum of Sacred Art,

The Baptistry. Its architecture and mosaic decoration are in harmony with its function. In the background, above the little altar, there is a large mosaic representing the Crucifixion. The patron of these works was Doge Andrea Dandolo, who is buried there. He was a humanist and a friend of Petrarch. At the foot of the altar is buried Jacopo Sansovino, overseer of St. Mark's in the XVI century.

The mosaic decoration of the Baptistry shows traces of the sense of realism and of movement destined to characterize the art of the XV century.
The Magi, dressed in sumptuous oriental garments, bring presents to Jesus.

▶

St. Mark's Basilica plan of groundfloor.

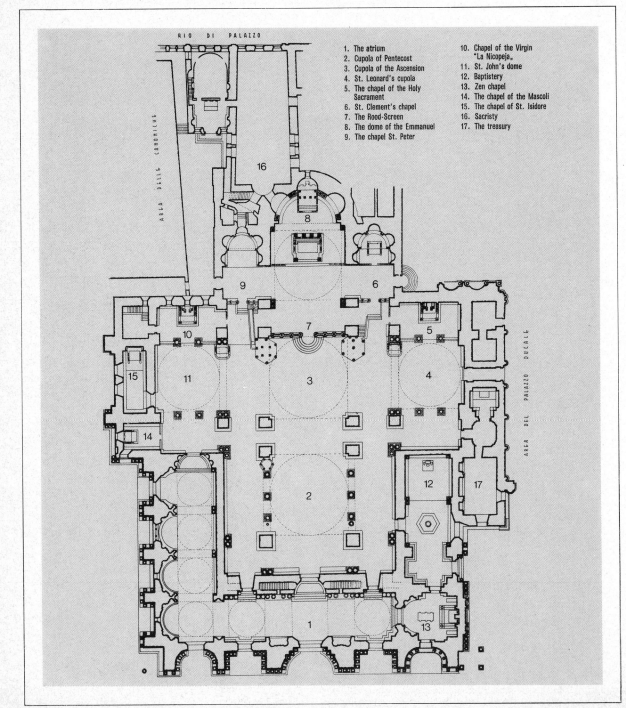

1. The atrium
2. Cupola of Pentecost
3. Cupola of the Ascension
4. St. Leonard's cupola
5. The chapel of the Holy Sacrament
6. St. Clement's chapel
7. The Rood-Screen
8. The dome of the Emmanuel
9. The chapel St. Peter
10. Chapel of the Virgin "La Nicopeja„
11. St. John's dome
12. Baptistery
13. Zen chapel
14. The chapel of the Mascoli
15. The chapel of St. Isidore
16. Sacristy
17. The treasury

REX · IDDEORVN ·

King Herod gives a banquet. Both the details and the whole are presented with a strangely modern sense of realism.

▶ Salome's dance (detail). Following her mother's advice she asks King Herod for John the Baptist's head as a reward for the dance. The original quality of the clothes, the vivid colours and the motions of her body make Salome a surprisingly expressive figure.
Even contemporary fashion has sometimes sought inspiration in this emblematic figure.

The four horses, decorating the façade and situated on the loggia in front of the upper great arch. They were placed here in the XIV century. This unique piece was moulded and cast in the Hellenistic age (IV century B.C.) and brought to Venice from Constantinople as a war trophy by Doge Enrico Dandolo in 1204. The monument is now being studied by the Istituto Centrale del Restauro.

The Ministry of Public Education, under the aegis of UNESCO, is going to entrust the matter to a group of international experts, who will give their opinion on the restoration and preservation of this priceless art treasure threatened by various kinds of atmospheric pollution.

▶
The flood of November 4th, 1966 gave further and incontrovertible proof that « high tides » and rough seas are a great danger to the safety of Venice. During the recent years the situation has become very serious. Solutions are now beng actively sought and opinions are often controversial.

This is a view of St. Mark's Square during the 1966 flood. The salt water covered the floor of the Basilica and filled the whole crypt up to the ceiling.

whose creation has been much talked about and hoped for during all these years, and is now practically a moral duty, if we think of all the sacred ornaments and objects of cult which have lately been stolen, given away or dispersed.

Instead of the Roman ritual the sacred liturgies followed a rite of their own, called « Patriarchino », which had originated in Grado and Aquileia. It differend from the Roman ritual in the colour of the sacred vestments and the variable parts of the Mass, in the way offices were said and processional psalms sung, in the prayers and ceremonies of the Holy Week and the administration of the Sacraments, in the funeral rites and in the Little Office. In the litanies the Virgin received an original salutation: « *Sancta Maria omnium fons armatorum* ». She was also honoured with a special *Te Deum*: « *Te Matrem Dei laudamus, te Maria Virginem confitemur* ». A moving moment during the ceremony of Baptism was when the godfather lay the little Christian child on the floor of the church while the *Pater Noster* was sung. In this way the child took possession of the church which became his new home. In St. Mark's the Epistle and the Gospel were sung till recently with modulations recalling those used in the East, and this style of singing was called « alla Patriarchina ».

Music and singing are an essential part of the rite, and St. Mark's has reached the status of an authority also in this field. Tradition has it that in 800 a certain Giorgio Veneziano, a priest, went up to Charlemagne's court in Aachen and offered to build an organ « *mirifica arte graecorum* ». What is certain is that since ancient times the Basilica has always taken the greatest care of its singers and players of all sorts of instruments, even the most strange, as well as of its organs and its maestri, who were responsible for the decorum of the executions. In 1491 the Maestro di Cappella was given absolute power, and all the singers, players and organists had to obey him. To enlarge upon the Marciana Chapel would be tantamount to writing the history of music. One name is enough, Claudio Monteverdi, who added so much lustre to it.

At the turn of the last century Maestro Lorenzo Perosi was invited by Patriarch Giuseppe Sarto to become the conductor of the Marciana Chapel. He was destined to become also one of the pillars of the renovation of sacred music, which the church had decided upon in order to bring it back to its original purity and to the dignity proper to its function.

Patriarch Roncalli wanted to honour the memory of the Maestro with a lapidary inscription situated at the foot of the Ponte di Canonica, beneath the windows of the rooms where Perosi once lived: « *...sacri cantus restitutor amplioris meliorisque famae — iter sibi munivit...* ».

In 1899 Pope Leo XIII called him to Rome to become the conductor of the Sistine Chapel. It is said that during an audience the Pope asked Perosi whether he was sorry to leave Venice: « Very sorry », answered don Lorenzo, « and above all to have to part from my Patriarch ». « Do not worry », the Pope is supposed to have answered, « you will go on serving your Patriarch ». It was a vaticination that Cardinal Sarto would wear the tiara.

In 1953 I met Maestro Perosi at the Basilica of Massenzio in Rome, where he was conducting one of his oratorios, « The Nativity of the Redeemer ». I told him that the Venetians remembered him with affection and nostalgia, and invited him, in the name of my city, to come to Venice to direct one of his oratorios. He was very happy to accept the invitation and promised he would conduct « The Resurrection » at La Fenice Theatre towards the end of that year, in memory of Pope Sarto, who had recently been canonized. Everything had been organized, but then at the last moment the conditions of the Maestro's health defeated the noble purpose.

Some years later, in 1956, Maestro Igor Stravinsky conducted a vocal-instrumental concerto in the Basilica of St. Mark, the « *canticum sacrum in honorem Sancti Marci* », which he had composed for the occasion. The Basilica was full to bursting point and the ambient created a strange kind of suggestion; many showd signs of almost paroxysmal exaltation; many were like stunned. I left St. Mark's feeling as if somebody had dealt me a blow on the head. There is no doubt that that night Venice lived one of her most intense experiences.

These are touches of real life and manners which give a quickening vibration to what is our great theme: the Basilica of St. Mark.

Death in Venice. Such an event is unconceivable. The classical world believed that a city would die if its Palladium was lost or stolen. St. Mark's is our Palladium, and no attempt will be made on the Basilica: « *in cordibus nostris non moriere Leo* ».

It is true that many things conspire against Venice, and among them I would include also the sloth and malevolence of men, but I am confident. The whole world loves Venice, for the city is a unique reality in the history of civilization, and this fills us with hope and courage. Beneficence may be a welcome sign of solidarity, but it is we the Venetians and we the Italians who must take the helm into our hands and steer the right course.

Under the seating of an arch on the external wall of the tower-shaped building where the Treasure is kept there are two stealthily carved *putti* bearing a label with an inscription in Venetian dialect: « l'om po far e die in pensar — e vega quelo che li po' incontrar » (loosely: let us be ready for whatever the future has in store); it is a warning of all times for all times.

And what shall we do against the forces of evil? In the School of St. Mark there is a large painting in the style of Giorgione: on a stormy night like that of November 4, 1966 St. Mark delivers Venice from a ship full of devils. Let us wait for the new miracle.

EUGENIO BACCHION
PRIMO PROCURATORE DI SAN MARCO

INDEX OF ILLUSTRATIONS

Terza Edizione
P. Marzari/Industrie Grafiche s.r.l./Schio/Italy
Design Luigi Pagliani